FAITHFULLY

HIS

*Ms. Linda,
May God's goodness surround you
in new ways in this season! He
sees you and knows!
— Cierra & Cotter*

FAITHFULLY

HIS

A Journey of Discovering the Unfailing
And Unconditional Love of God

Cierra Rebekah Cotton

Copyright 2020 © Cierra Rebekah Cotton
ISBN: 978-0-692-15778-7

All rights reserved. This book or parts thereof may not be reproduced in any form, stored in any retrieval system, or transmitted in any form by any means—electronic, mechanical, photocopy, recording, or otherwise—without prior written permission of the publisher, except as provided by United States of America copyright law.

Unless otherwise noted, Scripture quotations are taken from the New King James Version. Copyright © 1979, 1980, 1982 by Thomas Nelson, INC. Used by permission. All rights reserved.

Scripture quotations marked NLT are taken from the Holy Bible, New Living Translation, Copyright © 1996, 2004, 2007 by Tyndale House Foundation. Used by permission of Tyndale House Publishers, Inc., Carol Stream, Illinois 60188. All rights reserved.

Scripture quotations marked ESV are from The Holy Bible, English Standard Revision® (ESV®), Copyright © 2001 by Crossway. Used by permission. All rights reserved.

Scripture quotations marked AMP are taken from the Amplified® Bible (AMP), Copyright © 2015 by The Lockman Foundation. Used by permission. All rights www.Lockman.org

Scripture quotations marked NASB are taken from the New American Standard Bible® (NASB), Copyright © 1960, 1962, 1963, 1968, 1971, 1972, 1973, 1975, 1977, 1995 by The Lockman Foundation. Used by permission. www.Lockman.org

Cover Design by MC20 Design, LLC.
Printed in the United States of America.
First printed edition 2020.

Cierra Rebekah Cotton
1914 Skillman Street, Suite 110-147,
Dallas, TX 75206
www.cierrarebekah.com

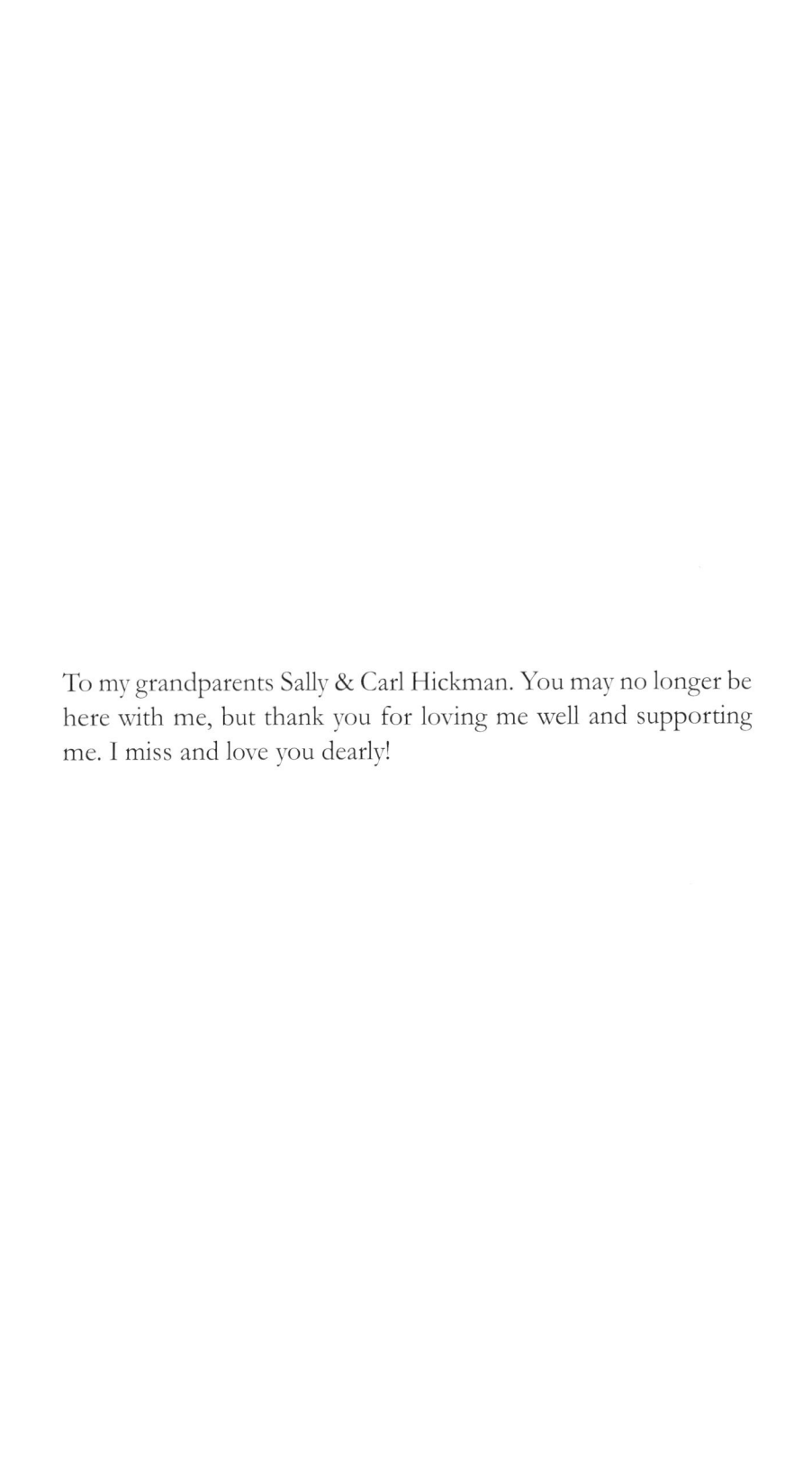

To my grandparents Sally & Carl Hickman. You may no longer be here with me, but thank you for loving me well and supporting me. I miss and love you dearly!

TABLE OF CONTENTS

Acknowledgements 1
Introduction 3
Opening Prayer 11

Part 1: Love Redefined 13
Chapter 1: What is Love? 15
Chapter 2: God's Demonstration of Love 25

Part 2: Identity Crisis 39
Chapter 3: Who am I? 41
Chapter 4: Who Does God Say I Am? 53
Chapter 5: Death to The Cookie Cutter Christian 67

Part 3: The Process 79
Chapter 6: Set Free 83
Chapter 7: Finding Security in God's Grace and Love 101

Part 4: On Mission 113
Chapter 8: Created for Purpose 115
Chapter 9: Fulfilling God's Purpose and Mission 123

Part 5: Resting in God's Faithfulness 131
Chapter 10: What has God Promised? 135
Chapter 11: Trusting God When He Says "No" 147
Chapter 12: Fear Not 157

Part 6: Enduring the Valley 165

Chapter 13: Trusting God in Seasons of Hardship 167
Chapter 14: Remaining Faithful Through Suffering 177
Chapter 15: Do Not Give Up 185

Part 7: Faithful in Every Moment 193

Chapter 16: Prayer: The Ultimate Love Language 195
Chapter 17: Moving Forward 205

Notes 213
About the Author 217

ACKNOWLEDGEMENTS

Thank you, Brittney, for believing in me and speaking life when I wanted to give up, speak death, or believe the lies of Satan.

Thank you, Deitra, for praying for me. It was literally your prayers that allowed me to even be able to publish this book. You are my sister forever, and I thank God for you.

Lisa, your belief in the power of prayer has encouraged me on so many levels. Thank you for praying for me and keeping me lifted day in and day out.

My Saturday prayer circle, you all are absolutely amazing, and I thank you for your continual willingness to show up and share your hearts.

Thank you to countless other friends, co-workers, and family who believed in me when I didn't. May God bless you richly for pouring into me throughout this process.

Mom and Dad, thank you for raising me in the Lord so that, when I grew older, I had a solid foundation to stand upon. I love you!

INTRODUCTION

Before I knew what love was, He loved me.
Before I knew who He was, He had already claimed me as His own.
Before I ever knew I needed to be forgiven, He had already sent His Son to die for me.
Before I took a breath of life, He had already been busy at work planning the life He wanted me to live.

Those important truths have become the foundation for my life, but that wasn't always the case. There have been many times in my life where I felt abandoned, heartbroken, disappointed, or unloved. Moments when I wanted to end my life because of how depressed and alone I felt. Periods of time when I felt trapped and unable to fully express my feelings to others. Seasons in which I lived a defeated life without a real sense of freedom. Years spent suffering in silence behind the smile on my face while just praying on the inside that someone—anyone—would take notice and help me.

Well, unfortunately, no one on this earth ever did.

But someone even better stepped in and took notice of me. In fact, ever since my birth, He has never taken His eyes off me. His name is Jesus Christ, and He has completely transformed me from the inside out. If it weren't for His constant display of grace, mercy, and unconditional love, I would not still be here. I am completely thankful that He saw something in a little girl from Baltimore, Maryland and gave me a voice and a platform upon which to share His truth and love with a dying and lost world. I owe everything to Him, and I will live the rest of my life doing everything I can to give Him the glory and honor that He deserves because He rescued me from the power of sin, bondage, self-destructive thoughts, and heartache that used to be a part of my everyday life.

This book is about my journey of awakening to the truth that there is nothing that could ever separate me from the love of God (Romans 8:39) and finding security in His offer of salvation. This quest of discovery led me to realize that He is too great, too powerful, and too loving to throw me away when I make a mistake or sin against Him. In fact, it is His grace and mercy that keep me day after day, year after year. Saying "yes" to following Jesus means that I am His forever. Why is that?

Because I didn't choose Him; He chose me.

In fact, the more I meditated on His truth, the more I became aware of my true identity in Christ. My eyes were opened to see that I could boldly approach God as His daughter rather than approaching Him as a fearful stranger. I could be honest with Him about how I was feeling, express my shortcomings, and be confident that His unconditional love for me never changes. Actually, it is my faith in His unconditional love that now secures and sustains me even through the hardest moments in life.

If you are anything like me, then you have at one time or another questioned if God truly does love you or if He truly

INTRODUCTION

cares about you. Maybe He did not answer a prayer in the way you thought He would, or maybe He allowed a difficult trial in your life that left you confused and discouraged. It is okay to admit that you doubt or question God at times because, truth be told, we all do. And you know what? God is not intimidated by your weakness or questions. During those moments, our faith has a chance to grow, and God is able to reveal Himself to us in new ways if we turn to and seek Him all the more. As long as we are on this side of heaven, we are going to be tempted to not believe the truth about God, especially when hard times come. That is why it is so important for us to take time to get to know the character of God through His Word and meditate on His promises as a weapon to combat the lies that surround us.

Some of the questions that my peers and I have grappled with are:

- Why does God love me?
- Can I be sure that God loves me?
- Do I have to earn God's love?
- How can I believe that God loves me when I am struggling to pay my bills?
- If God loves me, why did my cousin get shot by the police?
- If God is good, why do bad things happen to good people?
- Why do I feel so alone if God is supposed to always be with me?
- If God is sovereign, why is my husband filing for divorce?
- Why did God allow me to have a miscarriage?
- If God is so loving, why do I feel so unloved?

I did not discover God's unfailing and unconditional love overnight, nor did it come naturally for me to grasp it. In fact, I'm still in the process. It took a season of unemployment and a housing eviction for me to fully begin to realize the extent of His love. The Lord used that time to show me that walking in obedience will not always result in the outcome that I might desire, but His purpose will always prevail. I also had to come face-to-face with the fact that I am a flawed individual who makes mistakes, but I serve a God whose love covers me even in the midst of the valley.

You see, I grew up in the church, sang the songs, and attended Sunday School, yet I still questioned the depth of His love for me. I admit that I have wrestled with the idea of whether or not His love equates to goodness, especially at times when my life was not "good." This faulty view of God caused me to be insecure and ask questions like the ones above. But isn't it typical of us to feel loved and blessed when life is going well? However, as soon as we witness evil or suffering in our lives or the lives of others, our first reaction is often to question God's faithfulness.

Surely, if God truly loved us, we would never face trials and tribulations, right?

Wrong. Nothing could be further from the truth. Throughout the Scriptures, we see countless examples of God disciplining, maturing, and pruning through suffering and hardship those whom He loved. The Bible illustrates plenty of examples of people who suffered even though they did not do anything wrong. We have to trust and believe that, even in our pain and suffering, God still loves and has His eye on us. If we took time to examine

INTRODUCTION

our hearts, we would discover that, when we question God's love, we are really questioning His character. Every day, we have to make a choice to believe what God's written word says over our feelings and emotions. We may not always feel loved, but we can't base the Lord's love for us on temporal issues and problems; we must look to the cross. It is at the cross that we can find safety, refuge, peace, hope, forgiveness, rest, love, and freedom.

It is my desire for you to know that no matter what you may face in this lifetime:

1. *God sees you (Psalm 33:13-15, Psalm 139:15-18).*
2. *God cares for you (1 Peter 5:7).*
3. *God is with you (Deuteronomy 31:8).*
4. *God loves you (Romans 5:8, John 3:16).*
5. *God knows what you are going through (Psalm 139:1-6, Hebrews 4:13).*

If you are perfect and never face any challenges, then this book isn't for you. In fact, if that's you, I would love us to sit down with a cup of tea and figure out your secret!

This book is for those who recognize that they are in need of God's grace. For those who have questions about God and are curious to know if He is real. For those who are new in their faith and want to go deeper. For those who are mature in their faith but might be having trouble believing God right now. For those who have, at one time or another, questioned whether or not God truly loves them. For those who are willing to be honest about where they are in life and are open to God changing their hearts. For those whose lives have been transformed by the gospel but seem to be having trouble truly overcoming their past. For those who are in the midst of a storm and need to be reminded of the sovereignty of God. For those who want to experience the FREEDOM that God has promised us as His children. If you fit any of those categories above, then you are in the right place!

No matter your background, no matter your skin color, no matter your age, no matter your gender, the Lord has created you in His image and desires to have an intimate, personal relationship with you. He desires for you to know Him and experience His love. I don't believe that you picked up this book by chance, because I trust that my God is detailed and intentional. He allowed you to read this because He has something for you to gain from the words on these pages. My prayer is that God will meet you where you are and correct any false ideologies you may have believed about Him, others, or yourself along the way.

I don't know where you are in life, but my prayer is that, through my testimony and the truth found in the Scriptures, your eyes would be opened to discover how deep, how high, how long, and how wide God's love is for you (Ephesians 3:18). If you are a believer, I want you to be confident that you are God's child, no matter what storms may come or how you feel. God saved you by His grace when you put your faith in Christ. Your daughtership/sonship is not contingent upon how long your quiet time is on any given day or how many good deeds you perform. Your salvation is founded on and secured through Christ and Christ alone.

If you have never placed your faith in Jesus as your personal Lord and Savior, my prayer is that your eyes and heart will be

INTRODUCTION

opened to see just how good, faithful, and true He really is. I pray that you would accept the invitation that God is laying before you to become a part of His family forever by believing in His Son, Jesus Christ. And I want you to know that His death on the cross for your sins truly paid the debt that you owed forever. So, go grab your favorite mug, pour yourself some tea or coffee, and let us dive in together.

Shall we begin?

OPENING PRAYER

Here is my heart, Lord; I surrender to You.

Father, I pray for all of those who shall lay hold of this book and read it. I ask that you open their eyes to see Your unfailing & unconditional love for them, through Jesus Christ. Draw them closer to Your heart, and may they find true rest in You. I pray that if anyone is doubting or questioning their faith, You would use this book to shatter all the misconceptions they have of You. Holy Spirit, minister to Your people and lift them out of the guilt and condemnation of their pasts. Set them free from the lies of society and Satan so that they may be made whole. Show them who You truly are and who they truly are in You. I pray that chains would be broken and that Your children would be transformed by the renewing of their minds with the truth of Your word. May we rise up out of the ashes as victors instead of victims, declaring that You are good and faithful. Daddy, use them as instruments of mercy and light in this dark and perverse world. I dedicate this book to You and pray that every word written would be inspired by the Holy Spirit.

In Jesus' Name,
Amen

Part 1

LOVE REDEFINED

1
WHAT IS LOVE?

"And we have known and believed the love that God has for us. God is love, and he who abides in love abides in God, and God in him."
1 John 4:16 NKJV

I still remember it like it was yesterday. I was in high school the first time a guy told me that he loved me. I had just gotten out of my last period class, American Government, and was heading to my locker to drop my books off and head home. As I exited the classroom, he was waiting for me with a big smile on his face. He had quickly become one of my closest friends at school and just always seemed to be around at the right time. I smiled back and like a typical high school girl, greeted him like I had not just seen him before my last class began.

I said "goodbye" to my friends as he and I walked down the hallway together to the stairs. My locker was on the lower level, which meant walking down six flights of stairs that were quite chaotic as students were rushing to go home. Once we passed the first floor, where everyone else was rushing to exit, we found ourselves alone. Before we could reach the lower level, he stopped me in the stairwell, gazed into my eyes, and expressed his admiration and love for me. My legs felt weak, and it seemed as if everything was happening in slow motion.

This was it.

This is what I saw portrayed in all the romantic movies that I watched. There were butterflies in my stomach, and my heart was beating so fast. Then, he said those three sacred words, "I love you." Immediately, my eyes lit up, and a huge smile spread across my face. As he continued to express why he was interested in me, I couldn't help but think that this was the best moment of my life. Being the young and naïve teenage girl that I was, I didn't know the impact that those words would have on my life. I spent the next few weeks on cloud nine and in awe of the fact that a guy—a cute guy at that—had actually told me that he loved me. I was so excited to hear those words because, at that point in my life, not many male figures affirmed me in that way. Now, I wouldn't have been able to articulate it in that way back then. But looking back on it now, I know that's exactly what was happening.

As our friendship grew, I became convinced that he was going to be someone pretty special in my life for a really long time. It felt great to be chosen, sought after, adored, and to have someone who would listen to me. Sadly, that moment was short-lived, as the actions of my pursuer did not match up with the words that he spoke on that day in the stairwell. Eventually, my heart was broken and left shattered in pieces. The romantic picture of love that was portrayed in the media didn't look anything like the story of my life. I began to question if true love really even existed as I looked at the relationships in my family and circle of friends.

In the weeks and years to come, I began to realize that most people will tell you what you want to hear in an effort to get you to do what they want. They will casually say words without truly understanding the weight of them. I had such a strong desire to feel special that it didn't take much for my interest in a guy to grow. My parents had a rule that I couldn't date until I was 21, but that didn't stop me from talking to a few guys and getting emotionally involved with them. It would be a few more years before I realized that the love I was searching for in another human to fulfill and complete me could only be found in a relationship with my Heavenly Father.

Love.

It is a word that a lot of us use on a daily basis, but do we really know exactly what it is? Does love even exist, or is it just a word that comes and goes? Does love abandon, or does it mean commitment until the end? Is there an expiration date on love? Is there a difference between the love of God and the love we receive from other people?

For you personally, what immediately comes to mind when you hear the word "love"? A family member? A spouse? A friend? Have you ever counted how many times a day you said you loved someone or something? In our society, love is a word that tends to come and go. It has become something that we use to describe people, places, and things that we like a lot, but like and love are two different concepts that we often confuse. Like is a feeling, while love is a decision. Typically, we say we love these people, places, and things because of the benefits or pleasure we receive from them. Once we no longer see the benefits from those people, places, and things, we often stop loving them.

We love food. We love sports teams. We love our family. We love our neighborhood. We love our culture. We love movies. We love our church. And there's nothing wrong with any of those things. It's quite natural for us to have preferences towards certain things, but as believers, we are called to a higher standard of love. This love is not based upon our feelings, preferences, or emotions. It is a conscious decision to put the well-being of others before ourselves, a greater love that, unfortunately, not everyone has had a chance to experience or see. This greater demonstration of love is based on the deliberate choice of the one who loves rather than the worthiness of the one who is loved. This is *agape* love. I once heard Dr. Tony Evans of Oak Cliff Bible Fellowship Church put it this way, "Biblical *agape* love is a decision, regardless of an emotion."[1] It is a love that only our Heavenly Father could reveal to us. Without Him, we are incapable of even demonstrating this type of love to others.

The *agape* love of God is unconditional and will not abandon you. It always has your best interest in mind. It looks at you in your most depraved state and still reaches out to pursue you. This love desires for you to walk in freedom from sin and fights for you. It is sacrificial and desires to walk in intimate fellowship with you and me. This love has prepared a way for us to spend eternity by His side, and it requires us to forsake our modern-day idols and pursue truth. This love requires us to recklessly abandon ourselves to love our enemies and allows for us to be made whole. This love comforts us in the weakest and lowest moments. This love casts out fear; it brings hope, produces peace, and ultimately unites.

WHAT IS LOVE?

This love is found in and through Jesus alone.

"For God so loved the world that He gave His only begotten Son, that whoever believes in Him should not perish but have everlasting life."
John 3:16 NKJV

This topic of love has been on my heart for a few years now as I have sought to understand God more. All throughout the Scriptures, we see God's pursuit, protection, provision, and even pruning of people as an expression of His love. It was love that prompted Him to send Jesus to the cross, and it was love that caused Jesus to rise from the grave three days later. Yet, I still believe that we are prone to be deceived about the true definition of love.

Our culture screams at us every day that love is conditional and temporary, and it's about getting your way and having your needs met. It's based upon how we feel about a particular person or thing, and since our feelings change, so does our love. Is this truly love, though? Is this the love that is described in the Bible? No, and it's this type of thinking that keeps so many of us in bondage.

You may be thinking, "Cierra, I am not in bondage. Speak for yourself!" But here's the thing: many of us have a theoretical understanding about love, but has your understanding of love changed the way you live your life? If not, then you are still in bondage (we will talk more about this in Chapter 6).

There is good news. The truth found in God's Word is powerful enough to help us break free from any and every bondage that keeps us from walking in true freedom. Our Heavenly Father wants us to be free to receive His love for us and to freely extend love to others. We need to ask The Lord to renew our minds through His word in order to discover what it means to be loved without limits. We are so accustomed to conditional love that it's often very hard for us to grasp that concept.

I have the amazing opportunity to work with young women and men at a community center, and many of the issues they are facing revolve around this topic of love (or what they consider to be love). What I have found is that their lack of understanding of love has caused them to be confused, hurt, lonely, and heartbroken. They fight, cheat, gossip, and slander all in the name of what they "love." Their identity is wrapped up in who or what they "love" instead of being rooted in Christ. The "love" they pursue is temporal and fleeting and stops once the benefit is gone. Let me just say that I completely understand their point of view because I can relate. Until the Lord began to open my eyes and changed my perspective, I was just like them. In fact, I have to continually renew my mind in this area because the culture that we live in promotes a viewpoint of love that is the polar opposite of what God teaches us about love.

> *The Merriam Webster Dictionary* defines "love" in this way:
> *Strong affection for another arising out of kinship or personal ties.*
> *Attraction based on sexual desire.*
> *Affection based on admiration, benevolence, or common interests.*
> *The object of attachment, devotion, or admiration.*[ii]

In the 21st century, many believe that love has to be earned, that it's an emotion or a feeling. And some, because of the narrative surrounding them, don't even believe that it exists. However, we are commanded as believers to "love one another" (John 13:34-35). So, if we have been commanded to "love one another," then love must exist, and it must be something that is attainable for us all.

WHAT IS LOVE?

While writing this book, I turned to my social media accounts and asked two questions:

1. What comes to mind when you hear the word "love"?
2. How has that changed since you came to know the Lord, ddif you are a believer?

I got a variety of responses ranging from:

- Kisses and hugs
- Devotion
- Compassion
- Sacrifice
- Self-love
- Self-less
- Relationship with your parents, spouse, or children
- Unconditional
- Vulnerability
- Forgiving
- Passion
- Best friend
- Peace
- Comfort
- Genuine
- Loyal
- Caring
- Mattered
- Sweet
- Safety
- Everlasting
- My Boyfriend

I also received a few comments on this topic:

"Without reservation; fully committed. Yes, it's changed since I became a disciple. I used to believe that I had to earn someone's love." -Nikkei L.

"Love used to be a feeling, but when I came to know God, I noticed that it's more [of an] action because it needs to exist when I feel like being loving, and it still [needs] to exist when I don't feel it." -Tasha A.

"[At first] hugs and kisses but now love means whole-hearted care and selfless concerns." -Joanbiya F.

"At first I thought love was an emotion felt between two people... Now that I have come to know Christ, I realize that love is something much stronger. Love is full of sacrifices because God sacrificed Jesus for us. Being that I realize the depth of love (according to what God allows me to understand), I can love others better because Christ loves me." -Arielle B.

"When I was younger love meant being in a relationship and getting attention. I didn't know what it really was; I only had an idea of how I wanted it to feel. Since being saved that love is not based on emotions or people, but it's Jesus dying for me. And love is WHO God is...patience, kindness, goodness, faithfulness, joy, peace, etc." -Kamri P.

As I read through the responses, I began to realize that I wasn't the only one that had, at one point, been deceived and wrong about the definition of love. A lot of us probably assumed we knew what the definition of love was based on what we learned from watching television shows and movies, from listening to music, or from what was demonstrated to us by our family. The more I read the Scriptures and continue on this journey of faith, the more I am convinced that love is an action that is not dependent upon my feelings or emotions but upon my relationship with Jesus Christ. I don't have to be best friends with a person to love them. I don't even have to know them to love them. But if I do want to walk in authentic love, I need to have a relationship with the One who initiates love. There is no true love apart from His. According to 1 John 4:19 (ESV),

"We love because He first loved us."

What conclusion can we draw from this Scripture reference? Our ability to love God and others is made possible because He loved us first. Apart from Christ, we are incapable of knowing God's plan for love, nor would we be able to extend His love to others. Have you ever heard the expression, "you can't give what you don't have?" Well, it's true. If we haven't received the love of Christ, we will not be able to love others the way He has commanded us to in His word. Instead, we will settle for one of the cheap imitations that our culture has created.

The love that God has called us to as believers is *agape* (we will discuss this more in the next chapter). This love is unfailing, relentless, perfect, and unconditional. It looks past the faults and shortcomings of others and sees the good. This love is not just words spoken but involves sacrifice and commitment. It is not dependent upon the person's actions but upon the fact that we were all made in the image of God. This love was demonstrated for us at the cross when Jesus laid His life down for the world. As we move forward, I challenge you to take a moment to reflect on your beliefs about love.

Time to Reflect
1. What does love mean to you?
2. What circumstances or events have shaped the way you think about love?
3. What examples of love do you see being portrayed in the culture that are contrary to the *agape* love of God?

"He who does not love does not know God, for God is love."
1 John 4:8 NKJV

2

GOD'S DEMONSTRATION OF LOVE

"But God demonstrates His own love towards us, in that while we were still sinners, Christ died for us."
Romans 5:8 NKJV

What if I told you that, right now, at this very moment, you are loved more than you will fully be able to understand?

Yes, you.

No matter your background or past, God's love for you has no limits. In fact, according to Ephesians 3:18, it is "high, deep, wide, and long." At some point in your life, I am sure that you had someone tell you that God loves you, but are you fully convinced of that truth? Do you understand what God sacrificed in order to demonstrate that love towards you? It's not enough to know that we are unconditionally loved by God; we must live like we are unconditionally loved by God. This doesn't happen overnight.

We are all on a daily journey of choosing to believe truth rather than the lies of this world and Satan. It is a process that requires time, trust, and belief, as the truth about God's unfailing and unconditional love goes from being merely head knowledge to regenerating heart knowledge.

Hollywood paints many pictures of what love is and what it's supposed to look and feel like. We live in a society that is obsessed with an idea of love that is completely opposite of what the Bible shows us. Women give their bodies to men to whom they aren't married in exchange for "love." We have television shows and movies that highlight extra-marital affairs and glamorize the idea of one-night stands. Our music depicts men and women who enter in and out of many relationships in the name of "love." Cheating and pleasing oneself has become the norm, and our idea of love is so faulty that it often becomes hard for us to even truly believe that God's love is unconditional. Thankfully, we have the Scriptures to show us how God loves His people and how He has called us to love each other.

All of us—myself included—are wired for intimacy, community, and fellowship. We weren't created to live this life alone. To some degree, we all want to feel like we belong and are valued by another. Unfortunately, many of us settle for the cheap imitations that this world throws at us instead of seeking out the love of God. We settle for temporal pleasure instead of focusing our affections on the eternal love the Lord offers us. There are many Christians today who are looking for love, fulfillment, and satisfaction in all of the wrong places. We can recite John 3:16 forwards and backwards, but we don't allow that verse to transform the way we search for, give, and/or receive love.

How do I know? Because that was my story growing up. Instead of finding fulfillment in the Lord, I sought it in friendships, relationships, dance, school, and other meaningless things.

I grew up as the oldest of three girls in Maryland on the outskirts of Baltimore City. Growing up, church was like my second home. In fact, some of the earliest and fondest memories of my childhood occurred at a small, multi-cultural church in Owings Mills, Maryland. Missing church was not an option in the Cotton household. As a child, I knew that every Sunday and Wednesday meant that we were going to be in the house of the Lord. On the Sundays we missed church services due to sickness or family vacations, I cried. My environment created a solid foundation for me to hear the gospel at a young age and make a decision to surrender my life to Jesus. I enjoyed learning about God from the Bible and starting my days in the basement of our home worshipping to a Ron Kenoly VHS alongside my mom and sisters. My mother decided to homeschool us and was careful to give us the best Christian education that she could afford. My grandmother was a praying woman, and to this day, my great aunts serve the Lord faithfully. In those early years, I was surrounded by mostly Christian friends, and Vacation Bible School was one of the highlights of my summer. Basically, I was a church girl who was very excited about the things of God (if I were in public school, I probably wouldn't have been very popular).

Despite this solid foundation in the Lord, it wasn't until the age of 27 that I actually began to understand the depth of God's love for me. And not just for me but His creation in general.

It wasn't until the Lord brought me into a "wilderness season" that I finally began to open my heart to receive and embrace the fullness and tenderness of God's love. What do I mean by that? It's quite possible to go to church, know all the right Scriptures, pray, serve in the church, and even give an offering—yet not fully grasp the importance of Jesus' death on the cross. It is easy for us to sincerely say "yes" to Jesus regarding our eternal salvation but then shut Him out of other areas of our lives.

For most of my teenage life, that was my narrative. Although the foundation laid for my life was Christ-centered, it all came to a halt during my early adolescent years. Financial issues led to family issues, which led to marital issues, and being a part of a local church body no longer became a priority for us. I was no longer being given the opportunity to learn about God from mature men and women of God. I no longer had friends who challenged me to do the right thing. I no longer had a support system that discipled and modeled Christ-likeness for me. My heart grew cold, and my affections slowly faded away from the Lord without me even recognizing it as I navigated through high school and college.

I still occasionally went to church and prayed before every meal, but my heart was growing further and further away from God. As guys played with my emotions and professed their "love" for me, but then dumped me, my heart was broken. Instead of turning to God, I turned to teen magazines, television, and my peers for advice and comfort. Now, if you had asked me during that period of my life about my faith, I would have told you that everything was good, but it was not. Why? For the longest time, I didn't even realize I had yet to, or needed to, give God my whole heart.

The section of my heart full of hurt, disappointment, and fear was off limits to everyone, including God. I would pray and feel like God didn't hear me, which only added to my confusion and frustration. But you see, God was never the issue. My view of God was skewed. Once I began to dig into the Word of God for myself, He started to take the scales off my eyes. I began to see the Lord for who He truly is rather than who I thought He was. I began to see that it was His love that kept certain doors from opening in my life yet also opened certain doors for me. It was as if a light switch went off in my head as I finally began to grasp the healthy truth about God and His love.

This discovery didn't happen at one of the happiest moments of my life but one of the most disappointing ones—a moment where I discovered that nothing—not one thing—could ever separate me from His love. As I sat in my prayer closet crying out to God over the mess my life had become, He met me right where I was and began to show me that nothing I had ever done or would do could ever make Him love me any less or any more. He had loved me even when I was a sinner and an enemy of the cross. So now that I was following Him, I could rest in the security of the truth of His love. What is that truth?

God sent His Son to die for our sins so that we could be reconciled back to Him.

Do you believe that? I mean, do you *really* believe that enough to allow it to transform your life? The infinite God of the universe sent His one and only Son to die a criminal's death so that we might inherit eternal life. Jesus left His divine place of honor to come down to earth and show us just how much He loved us.

Our society paints many portraits of love, but none of them involve sacrificing oneself the way Jesus did at Calvary. Jesus didn't just die, though. He rose from the dead on the third day and then ascended into heaven 50 days later, leaving us with the gift of the precious Holy Spirit. This love story is so good that not even Hollywood could replicate anything close to what was demonstrated through Jesus' sacrifice. Once I began to understand the weight of His sacrifice and what I truly deserved, it changed the trajectory of my life.

There is no greater love than the love that God demonstrated through Jesus' death on the cross for our sake. He paid the ultimate price for our sins and gave us access to eternal life. His sacrifice also allows us to have fellowship and intimacy with God. You might be asking, "How is that love?" Well, when was the last time you watched a movie in which the superhero died for the villain? When was the last time you saw an innocent man willingly decide to take on the punishment of a criminal so that he or she could be free? That is exactly what Christ did for us at Calvary. He took the wrath of God that was meant for us so that we could be set free. Why? Because He loved us. In fact, when He went to the cross, He had you and me in mind, knowing that we would make mistakes, rebel at times, and disobey, yet He still went.

You might be thinking, "But I'm not a villain; I am a good person!" Romans 3:23 (ESV) would beg to differ:

GOD'S DEMONSTRATION OF LOVE

"For all have sinned and fall short of the glory of God."

Another way to phrase that is by saying that we all miss the mark. None of us is righteous on our own. We all say things that we shouldn't say, do things we shouldn't do, and think things we shouldn't think. Not one of us is capable of living a perfect and holy life apart from Christ. In fact, Psalm 51:5 tells us that we have all been born into sin. As humans, this sinful nature is a trait that we all inherit from birth, and it separates us spiritually from God. Why does this happen? Because of a poor choice that two people, Adam and Eve, made in the Garden of Eden.

You might be saying, "What does Adam & Eve have to do with me?" So let me give you the back story. Humankind has not always been spiritually separated from God. There was a brief period of time when sin was nonexistent and there was perfect harmony between God and humans. Now, for a moment, I want you to imagine being born into a perfect world. In this world, there is no death, no sickness, no taxes, no sorrow, no pain, no student loans, no turmoil, no war—it's just complete peace and order. You have the opportunity to dwell with the Lord, and there is nothing to separate you from His presence. He even walks and talks with you in the cool of the day. Sounds too good to be true, right? Well, that's the life that was created for Adam and Eve to enjoy in Genesis 1 and 2. God gave them everything they would ever need or want, and the only limitation they had was to not eat from the tree of the knowledge of good and evil. Adam and Eve had access to every other kind of plant, tree, and wildlife in the Garden of Eden. In fact, God had given Adam dominion, or complete rule, over all of it (Genesis 1:26).

One day, the Devil disguised himself in the form of a serpent to persuade Adam & Eve of the lie that God was withholding something good from them. He approached Eve first with this lie by turning God's command into a question in Genesis 3:1 (NKJV):

> "...And he said to the woman, 'Has God indeed said, "You shall not eat of every tree of the garden"?'"

She entered into a conversation with the Devil, which led to her doubt God's goodness and convince her husband, Adam, to believe the same. The Devil, with his slick and crafty ways, was able to convince them that if God was really good and loving, then they should be able to have access to everything and anything they wanted. He proposed and turned a command of God into an option and diminished God's Lordship in the process. Not once did the serpent mention all Adam and Eve could access from the garden and freely enjoy; he purposely focused on the one thing that the Lord had forbidden. Adam and Eve chose to give in to the serpent's temptation and committed the first sin by eating fruit from the tree of the knowledge of good and evil.

Even though Adam and Eve decided to disobey God (which led to them being separated from God's tangible presence), Genesis 3:15 shows us that from the beginning, God had a plan to reconcile us back to Himself. Fast forward thousands of years, and God's plan for His people was revealed in the sacrifice of His one and only Son for a rebellious group of people, including you and me.

GOD'S DEMONSTRATION OF LOVE

When we think of love stories, we think of movies like *The Notebook*, *Brown Sugar*, *The Best Man*, *Cinderella*, *Beauty and The Beast*, *Titanic*, and maybe even *Southside With You*, but there is absolutely no love story that could top the love that the cross displays for us.

"While we were still helpless [powerless to provide for our salvation], at the right time Christ died [as a substitute] for the ungodly. Now it is an extraordinary thing for one to willingly give his life even for an upright man, though perhaps for a good man [one who is noble and selfless and worthy] someone might even dare to die. But God clearly shows and proves His own love for us, by the fact that while we were still sinners, Christ died for us. Therefore, since we have now been justified [declared free of the guilt of sin] by His blood, [how much more certain is it that] we will be saved from the wrath of God through Him. For if while we were enemies, we were reconciled to God through the death of His Son, it is much more certain, having been reconciled, that we will be saved [from the consequences of sin] by His life [that is, we will be saved because Christ lives today]. Not only that, but we also rejoice in God [rejoicing in His love and perfection] through our Lord Jesus Christ, through whom we have now received and enjoy our reconciliation [with God.]"
Romans 5:6-11 AMP

Take a moment to reflect on that passage of Scripture and think about it this way: even if you were the only person on this earth, God would've still sent Christ to die on your behalf. That truth alone should cause us to offer up praise and thanksgiving to God! The fact that the Lord was willing to allow His wrath to be poured out on Jesus so that we could be declared innocent of our sins proves just how much He loves us. To think that an innocent man took on my punishment so that I could be reconciled back to God puts a smile on my face and joy in my heart. That's what I call love.

True love involves pain, discomfort, sacrifice, and denial of oneself all for the sake of another. God's love for us isn't dependent upon us being perfect and having it all together. It rests solely on the fact that He created us in His image. We are His masterpieces, and He has created us to bring glory and honor to His name. When we do not operate as though we are loved by the King of kings and The Lord of lords, we aren't able to love others well. Our low view of God's love causes us to become people who grumble and complain, instead of people who walk in a spirit of victory as overcomers by the blood of Jesus.

This is what I fear, though. We use the word love so loosely that when it comes to our relationship with God, we love Him the same way that we love food, sports, entertainment, etc. The word love is thrown around so casually today and is seen as something temporary. As we sit in church singing about love for God, it's hard for us to marvel in awe and wonder at His majesty because our terminology is the same as we use for things like chocolate. We rob God of the glory due to His name because our finite minds equate His love to the conditional love that we experience on this earth.

Another thing that the Lord has taught me is that we can't equate the love of God to how we are treated by other believers or how members of our local churches act. As humans, we will make mistakes and may not always treat each other according to the way God designed. The Church is full of flawed individuals who do not always love unconditionally or treat His image-bearers with the same value that God does. It can be hard, painful, and messy to love others who aren't perfect, but God makes it possible. He provides a way for us to look past the imperfections and forgive those who have hurt us through His love. As my pastor, Jerry Wagner, said in a sermon, "When unlimited forgiveness is experienced, then unlimited forgiveness is expected."[iiii] I'm not making an excuse for those who have wronged you, but I am saying that whatever they did to you is not greater than what Christ did for you at the cross. As believers, we have a choice to allow love to cover a multitude of sins (1 Peter 4:8) or to allow hatred to stir up conflict and strife.

"Hatred stirs up strife, But love covers all sins."
Proverbs 10:12 NKJV

We can say that we love God and others with our lips, but will we demonstrate that same unconditional love to others that God extends towards us when someone hurts us? Will we love freely and allow vengeance to truly be the Lord's (Romans 12:19)? Love and forgiveness will often be the harder choice, but it is the most freeing option as well. Choosing to forgive doesn't minimize what happened to you or mean that you have to pretend that nothing ever happened at all. Nor does it mean that you will not feel pain from the offense. It takes times to heal and rebuild trust and confidence in a broken relationship, and depending on the offense you might have to create boundaries to protect yourself. What it does mean is that, by God's grace, we resolve to not seek out revenge and trust that He will deal justly with our offender(s). It means that instead of holding a grudge or bitterness in our hearts we seek to forgive others the way that God has forgiven us. This is no easy task and we must pray that the Lord would help us to see people the way that He sees them, so that we can be set free. God's love for you and me equips us to love even those who seem unlovable.

It's hard for us as humans, at times, to understand the unconditional love of God because we are used to the human kind of love that we see modeled in the 21st century. Our love is fleeting and has the potential to change from one moment to the next. It is not stable, constant, or always faithful. In fact, many people may voice that they want a love that contains those qualities but will admit that it is hard to find. When we think of love, our minds don't always immediately begin to think about God first because we are bombarded with so many different ideas and depictions of love. In fact, Ancient Greeks believed that we are capable of expressing our love in at least seven different ways.[iv] As you read over the definitions in the chart below, I want you to think about which forms of love you see often practiced by society and the world around us. How many television shows, movies, magazines, or songs have you come across that actually showcase love in the way that God has defined it? I'm guessing that number is pretty low. There may be many different ways to categorize love, but God still calls us to love unconditionally whether we are relating to our family, friends, co-workers, neighbors, or classmates. To illustrate, I have organized

Neel Burton's ("These Are the 7 Types of Love" 2016) seven different definitions of love in the chart below:

Storge: natural affection; the love you share with your family
Philia: the love that you have for friends; esteem and affection found in a casual friendship.
Eros: sexual, physical, and erotic desire kind of love (positive or negative)
Philautia: the love of self (negative or positive)
Ludus: this is playful love; like childish love or flirting
Pragma: long-standing love; the love between a married couple
Agape: this is the unconditional love or divine love; a love that is based on the deliberate choice of the one who loves rather than the worthiness of the one who is loved[v]

The *agape* love found in Jesus is unlike anything we will ever experience from any earthly vessel, because it is divine, is sacrificial, eternal, and makes us whole. As believers, we have the opportunity to showcase this type of love to a world that is broken, lost, and without true hope. In fact, Jesus said that it was through our love for one another that the world would know we were His:

> *"By this all will know that you are My disciples, if you have love for one another."*
> *John 13:35 NKJV*

Although we may not always fully express *agape* love in our everyday interactions, we should never stop striving to love others in that way. Loving others unconditionally is hard, but we serve a God for whom nothing is impossible, which includes loving our enemies and those who hurt us. If we want to love others well, we must spend time in the presence of the One whom is love Himself. Once we do, loving others becomes a natural byproduct of our lives as we walk more in line with the Holy Spirit and less in line with our flesh (Galatians 5:16).

God is love. God is love. God is love. Often times, we hear of God's love for us so much that we become desensitized to what it truly means. Let us not forget that without His love, we would not be alive because the punishment we deserve is death. Let us thank God for creating a way for His love, forgiveness, mercy, and grace to be extended to us each and every single day. Let us seek to love others the way God has loved us.

Time to Reflect

1. What misconceptions about God's love have you believed?

2. What will you do differently now that you have a better understanding of God's unconditional love?

3. How will you move forward in being a distributor of God's love to others?

> *"Beloved, let us love one another, for love is of God; and everyone who loves is born of God and knows God."*
> *1 John 4:7 NKJV*

> *"A new commandment I give to you, that you love one another; just as I have loved you, you also are to love one another."*
> *John 13:34 NKJV*

Part 2

IDENTITY CRISIS

3

WHO AM I?

> *"… anyone who belongs to Christ has become a new person. The old life is gone; a new life has begun!"*
> 2 Corinthians 5:17 NLT

A few months ago, during a time of worship and prayer at work, I had a vision.

Now, I am not that person who receives visions and dreams often, so when I do, I try to pay close attention. What I saw was a flower surrounded by weeds and roots that were stunting its growth so much that it was hidden and barely able to survive. Then, a pair of hands came down from heaven and began pulling up the weeds and roots that were surrounding it. The more the hands dug up the weeds and roots, the more the flower began to bloom and come to life. The hands kept digging and digging until the weeds and roots around the flower were completely gone, and it stood fully bloomed and strong.

As I continued in prayer, I felt the Lord impressing upon my heart that He wanted to uproot all of the baggage, lies, and labels from the past that were falsely placed on His people so they would know that their true worth and identity is found in Him. He wanted to show His people who they were called to be in Him and free them from the lies of the culture, the society, and the world. Not only did He want to free them to see themselves how He sees them, but He also wanted to free them from any misconceptions about who He is. In essence, all of the things that we use to define ourselves that are outside of what He says, He desires to pull up in order to make room for us to bloom into the sons and daughters we are destined to be.

Why do I bring this up? Because there is an epidemic in our culture where many people—including believers—do not fully understand or even know in whom their identity lies. This is a problem because I believe that our impact on the world around us is limited when we don't walk in our true identity. You will hear me repeat this over and over again because it's such an important truth:

> *We have bought into the lie of our society that we are defined by what we do or what we possess, but our identity must be found in Whose we are.*

Some of us are struggling to find a sense of purpose in our lives because we are experiencing an identity crisis and trying to be someone that we weren't created to be. Others are trying to measure themselves by a standard that the Lord never set for them. As we move forward on this journey of discovering our true identity, I want you to answer a few questions.

WHO AM I?

What comes to mind when you hear the word "identity"?

Where has your identity come from?

Who or what has had the biggest influence on how you view your identity?

The *Merriam Webster Dictionary* defines an identity crisis as "a feeling of unhappiness and confusion caused by not being sure about what type of person you really are or what the true purpose of your life is."[vi] I believe that so many of the issues that we face here on this earth are tied to a lack of understanding our identity. We often struggle with comparing ourselves to others and aren't always satisfied with what we have been given because we aren't convinced of Whose we are. The Lord created you and me in His image and has given us an invitation of adoption into His family, yet we often live as orphans rather than as sons and daughters of God.

You are the Imago Dei!

This is a Latin term that simply means "image of God." We discover this truth in Genesis 1:26 (ESV),

> *"Then God said, 'Let us make man in Our image, according to Our likeness...'"*

Whether you like it or not, you bear the image and likeness of God. To put it simply, as our Creator, He has designed us to resemble Him mentally, morally, and socially. Although we were all created in His image, due to sin, we are not able to fully walk in our identity as His children until we place our faith in Jesus and become new creations in Him.

Without knowing you or your story, I can almost guarantee that at some point in your life, you went through a period of time when you questioned who you were supposed to be (for some of you, that might be where you are right now). You might have had parents who told you who and what they wanted you to be. Maybe you looked up to celebrities or leaders in your community. Or perhaps even the streets were the biggest influence in determining your identity.

The Word of God tells us in 1 Peter 2:9 that we are "chosen," "royal," "holy," and ultimately "His own special people," but what does that look like in our everyday lives? Many of us (even those raised in Christian homes) come to a point in our lives when what we heard in a church service doesn't match the reality we feel and see every day. For me, that happened during my high school and college years.

What I didn't realize then is that, apart from God, I would never discover my true identity. Instead, I unknowingly settled for carbon copies of what God had already imprinted on my soul and destined me to be. I wasted so many years trying to figure out something that the Lord already knew and desired to show me. Friends, we were made to glorify God and to reflect His image to the world. Some of us learn this the easy way, and some of us learn it the hard way.

Imagine waking up every morning and having to figure out which lie you are going to portray today. Imagine looking in the mirror and your first thoughts being, "I'm still not pretty enough, skinny enough, or good enough." Imagine believing that if you died, no one would even care. Envisioning yourself dying in a tragic car accident day after day with no one coming to your rescue. Contemplating suicide, but deep down inside, knowing you're just yearning for someone to see past the mask you wear to hide your inner pain. Putting on an act as if you are this perfect person, but your heart is full of pain, loneliness, and ultimately, brokenness. Finding your identity in school, dance, friends, random guys, and your hair. Spending most of your time trying so hard to please everyone else and gain their approval that you don't even know the real you.

If you haven't figured it out already, the person I described above used to be me. I believe the bulk of my insecurities started in the tenth grade when I first attended public school. I do not ever recall really doubting God's love or plan for me before then. But when I came face-to-face with the world, I struggled to find my identity amongst my peers as they would "jokingly" pick on me for "being different" or talk about the way I was raised.

It seemed as if I wasn't "black" enough to hang out with certain crowds and wasn't "white" enough to hang out with others. I was raised to speak standard English, but in this new environment, it was considered uncool. I wore clothes that were handmade, were from the thrift store, or were from places like Walmart & K-Mart, while a lot of my classmates wore Fubu, Sean John, Rocawear, Apple Bottoms, Baby Phat, & Ecko Red.

These differences made it very apparent that I didn't fit in with my new environment. As my eyes were opened to more trends and fads, I wasn't comfortable with myself, nor did I like myself. I hated my smile, my body's shape, and the way my nose looked. I used to have mini anxiety attacks all the time about my looks. I was constantly stressed out about what people thought of me. I didn't look like the girls in most of the movies, TV shows, or magazines, and I was trying to live up to some ideal standard of beauty that just isn't realistic. I hated looking at myself in the mirror and would sometimes wash my hands in the bathroom with the lights off just so I didn't have to look at myself.

My self-esteem was low, and it showed everywhere. In my dance classes, my teachers were constantly telling me to stop looking at the floor. Their singling me out only intensified the insecurities I was already feeling as a girl going through puberty trying to find my way through this world. I became emotionally guarded and a professional people-pleaser. I hated taking pictures of myself or being the center of attention. I grew up in a society that did not portray blackness—especially curly-kinky hair—as beautiful. Magazines featured blonde, blue-eyed girls with straight hair and super skinny frames, which caused me to think that my frame was abnormal. And I became so envious of that straight hair.

I felt like Pecola Breedlove, the main character from Toni Morrison's book *The Bluest Eye*[vii], who desperately wanted blue eyes because she thought they would make her beautiful. She looked to Shirley Temple as the epitome of beauty and believed that whiteness was beautiful and that she was ugly. I struggled to view myself as beautiful in a culture that did not showcase my physical features in a way that represented a standard of beauty. I had a lot of friends who truly believed that they were gifted, talented, and beautiful, but I could never seem to embrace those principles of truth.

What about you?

Who are you?

Why were you created?

What do you believe about yourself?

Where did those beliefs come from?

If you stripped away all of your possessions, titles, and accomplishments, what would be left?

I want you to take a minute to answer those questions above. Taking the time to examine how we identify ourselves is crucial to us becoming the women and men that God has created us to be. I have found myself having to go back to these same questions from time to time as God continues to shape me into His image. It's so easy to identify ourselves based on how others have labeled us rather than what's rooted in biblical truth. However, we cause great damage to our own personal and spiritual development and insult God's creative handiwork when we do.

I had labels placed on me as a child that kept me from dreaming bigger and taking risks. I quickly found that if I stayed within certain boundaries, then I avoided being ridiculed or embarrassed. Adapting to the culture around us is way easier than going against the cultural trends and habits. The problem with this assimilation is that the individual often loses their sense of personal identity along the way. They become someone that God never intended them to be so that they can fit the current temporal idea of what it means to be "popular," "accepted," or "right." That would be fine, except I don't believe God created us all to be the same. However, He did create us to all reflect the same person: Jesus Christ.

Our environment is often responsible for shaping how we ultimately view ourselves and the world around us. If we do not have anyone pointing us toward the truth found in God's Word, we will inevitably see ourselves through the lens of our community, neighborhood, society and/or the Enemy of our souls. We will identify ourselves based on what we see, hear, and experience instead of basing our identity on what God says about us.

I work with low-income students and families at a community center in an urban context. What I have observed over time is that many of them see themselves through the lens of their environment. Instead of describing themselves using character or personality traits, they describe themselves by what they do or where they are from. We took a group of students on a field trip to Prairie View A&M University, and there was one particular student who would not follow the behavioral expectations. He caused disruptions, wasn't focused, and kept goofing around. One of my coworkers later took him to the side to converse with him about his behavior, and it was revealed that he didn't see himself ever being able to attend college because he wasn't smart enough. His past behavior led people to label him as a "bad kid" who wasn't smart. He purposely did not behave well on the trip because as a "bad kid," he didn't feel like he would ever be good enough to fit in a college environment. Simply put, he mentally disqualified himself from an experience because he felt displaced and inadequate.

It is in our human nature to be quick to categorize and label. Early in our childhood education, we are taught to identify things by the way they look: their color, size, shape, characteristics, etc. We often fail to realize that, when it comes to the words we use to label other individuals, the impact of what we say is long-lasting. If someone tells me every day for the first ten years of my life that I am dumb, stupid, and good for nothing, then chances are that I will internalize it as truth. On the other hand, if someone tells me that I am smart, am intelligent, and have the ability to change the world for good, then chances are I will eventually believe it. It may take years, but as long as a person is consistent in speaking life over me, I will begin seeing myself in a positive way. The words that we choose to say about others are powerful and either create death or life in the hearts and minds of others (Proverbs 18:21). We are conditioned to see a person's behavior and then identify them by what they did or did not do, but how much more powerful would it be if we would commit to seeing people the way God sees them? What if we could be a part of a cultural revolution that helped people see that they were created in the image of the Almighty God so that they wouldn't feel the need to settle for the lesser versions of worth that currently flood our culture?

Lesser versions of worth are sure to create insecurities in us. As I mentioned in Chapter 2, we are born into sin and thus, begins the struggle to find our identity. Our sin nature is hardwired for us to believe the deceptive words of the Enemy about who we are, but the only way for us to uncover our true identity is to seek the One who created us. Until we seek Him, we will continue to be powerless to discover who we really are.

Growing up, I was subjected to many labels. Some of these labels accurately described my character and personality, while others held more negative connotations. I grew up believing that I was smart and could excel in school, but I didn't really see myself as beautiful. Why? It wasn't something that my parents mentioned a lot in our home. Now, I am not saying that they didn't think I was beautiful; it just wasn't a point of focus in our home. They were more concerned with building up my character and instilling good values over affirming my outer appearance. I eventually came to see myself as beautiful much later in college, but more importantly, I also came to understand the value of my identity in Christ.

Why is it so important that we know who we are in Christ? Because the way in which we identify ourselves determines how we approach life. If you find your value in achievements, you will have to continue to achieve more in order to feel worthy. If you find your value in possessions, you will have to accumulate more in order to feel worthy. If you find your value in titles, you will have to keep adding more positions to your resume in order to feel worthy. If you find your value in what people say, you will have to continue seeking approval from others in order to feel worthy. Seeking our value in all these different things leads to a cycle of bondage that robs us of the peace and contentment that is ours in Christ. I want you to be set you free today with the truth as revealed in God's Word. Are you ready?

You are not what you do.

You are not what others say or think about you.

You are not what others have done to you.

WHO AM I?

You are not your achievements.

You are not the things that you have done right or wrong.

For those of us who are in Christ Jesus, the old is gone and the new has begun. We are now identified as daughters and sons of God—not by any labels, achievements, past events, sins, gifts, or talents.

Time to Reflect
1. What have you tied your identity to?
2. Ask the Lord to reveal the areas in your life where you need to have your identity restored. Then ask Him to affirm your true identity as His daughter or son.

> *"See what kind of love the Father has given to us, that we should be called children of God; and so we are…"*
> *1 John 3:1 ESV*

4
WHO DOES GOD SAY I AM?

"And because we are his children, God has sent the Spirit of his Son into our hearts, prompting us to call out, 'Abba, Father.' Now you are no longer a slave but God's own child. And since you are his child, God has made you his heir." Galatians 4:6-7 NLT

Looking back over my high school and college years, I recognize how much of a HOT MESS I was. I know now that all of those feelings stemmed from me not knowing Whose I was. I didn't really like who I was because I placed my security and identity in everything and anyone except the only One who is the same yesterday, today, and forever: Jesus Christ (Hebrews 13:8).

I didn't have a true intimate relationship with God. I had a superficial one. Yes, I still prayed daily, went to church, and read my Bible, but it was mostly out of religious obligation rather than true devotion. Instead of renewing my mind with God's Word, I spent more time consuming media that supported materialism, greed, and perfectionism. The Devil was able to convince me that I was worthless and put so many crazy thoughts into my head because I wasn't putting on the full armor of God (Ephesians 6: 10-18) or casting down His lies (2 Corinthians 10:5). I was trying to find validation in people and things that couldn't fill the void that had grown so deep in my heart. And I was losing the battle daily.

I never felt good enough despite all my accomplishments in school, dance, and life in general. I was a National Honor Society-Dean's List-perfect attendance-scholarship-winning student who still felt empty. My greatest desire was to "fit in" and feel accepted, but no one ever knew it because I kept a smile on my face. I mean, not even my family or closest friends at the time knew how broken and lost I felt on the inside.

Eventually, in my early 20's, I reached my lowest point and couldn't take anymore. I was tired of putting on a façade. I was tired of feeling worthless and ashamed of who I was. I was tired of feeling enslaved to the opinions of others. I was tired of always trying to "fit in" and somehow always coming up short. It was at that point of full brokenness that I cried out to God—not in a church building or a Bible study, but in my bedroom. And you know what? He met me right there at that moment of surrender and immediately began to show me just how beautiful and precious I was to Him. He began to mend my heart and restore the joy that I had as a child. He began to restore the confidence that I lost somewhere during those teenage years.

It was such a new feeling.

"WHO DOES GOD SAY I AM?"

I had heard people compliment me all my life, but it wasn't until God Himself spoke to me and said, *"Cierra, I love you, and you are so beautiful to Me,"* that I actually believed it. My heart had been broken for so many years that hearing those words was like discovering a stream of cool water in the midst of a desert. I began to spend hours with God just basking in His presence and allowing Him to remove all the labels that I had accepted over the years that were completely contrary to the truth. As I studied the Scriptures with zeal and adoration, He showed me that before I was even born, He had a plan for my life. I wasn't a mistake. I had a purpose.

"For You formed my inward parts; You wove me in my mother's womb.
I will give thanks to You, for I am fearfully and wonderfully made;
Wonderful are Your works, And my soul knows it very well. My frame was not hidden from You, When I was made in secret, And skillfully wrought in the depths of the earth; Your eyes have seen my unformed substance; And in Your book were all written the days that were ordained for me, When as yet there was not one of them."
Psalm 139:13-16 NASB

Throughout high school and college, I had heard the powerful words in this beautiful text, but I did not listen to or believe them. My insecurities had made me desperate to fit in, but the whole time, God was calling me to be a light (which I hadn't fully comprehend in my youth). I didn't understand that, as a child of God, I am first and foremost His before I take on any other title. Who I am should establish what I do versus letting what I do establish who I am. So many times, we forget this simple truth: we are daughters and sons of God who have been given the opportunity to operate as wives, teachers, fathers, ministers, basketball players, business owners, hair stylists, bakers, CEOs, bankers, etc. Not the other way around.

Our true identity cannot be found in on our color, race, ethnicity, or culture. I am a Christian and a daughter of God first. In His design and sovereignty, The Lord delightfully decided that He wanted me to be an African-American woman who dances, loves serving youth, and currently works for a non-profit organization in Dallas, Texas. If my job title changed today, I would still be His daughter. If I could never dance again, I would still be His child. We must continually remind ourselves that our value is not in *what we possess* but in *Whose we are*. We are to work *from* our identity and not *for* our identity. God loves us enough to give us an identity rooted in Him. If we want to advance His Kingdom, we must remain rooted in Christ. We are called to influence and shift the culture—not to allow the culture to influence and shift us. The whole purpose of our existence is to make Christ known to a lost and dying world. This is an idea and lifestyle that is completely counter-cultural and foreign to our society. I stumbled across this quote while browsing the Desiring God website and it beautifully articulates the truth about our identity as Christians:

> *"Christian selfhood is not defined in terms of who we are in and of ourselves. It's defined in terms of what God does for us and the relationship he creates with us and the destiny he appoints for us. God made us who we are, so we could make known who he is. Our identity is for the sake of making known his identity."*
> -Author Unknown[viii]

Repeat this after me:

"WHO DOES GOD SAY I AM?"

I WAS CREATED TO MAKE KNOWN THE IDENTITY OF GOD.

When we are insecure about *who we are* and *Whose we are*, we tend to walk through life without a sense of purpose. Not understanding our purpose and calling is detrimental to our development as Kingdom individuals. Those who are insecure in their identity tend to be people-pleasers looking for affirmation from others. You could get drunk and high every single day or be the richest person in the world and own every single material possession that this world has to offer, but those things won't take care of your problems. At the end of the day, those things will only mask the emptiness you feel inside. That void is there because it can only be filled by our Creator.

If you place your identity or find your worth in anything other than Christ, you will always be disappointed. Why? Because when that person, position, or thing no longer exists or whenever there is an issue with it, you will end up feeling like you don't know who you are anymore. Placing your identity in something or someone that isn't eternal will eventually create an issue. The amazing thing about God is that we actually discover who we are created to be and what we are called to do when we seek Him. We don't have to guess or try to figure it out. He shows us step-by-step and frees us to be the unique individuals He designed us to be. We don't have to limit ourselves to the fleeting standard of this world. We can choose to stand upon Christ, the Solid Rock, and walk in the type of freedom and stability that lasts.

FAITHFULLY HIS

> *"But you are a chosen generation, a royal priesthood, a holy nation, His own special people, that you may proclaim the praises of Him who called you out of darkness into His marvelous light."*
> 1 Peter 2:9 NKJV

In this passage of Scripture, Peter, a disciple of Jesus, was writing to the Jewish Christians who had been scattered throughout Asia Minor and facing intense persecution. The Roman Empire was ruled by an evil emperor named Nero, who despised Christians and desired to rid Rome of them. Many Christians were being beaten, killed, and tortured because of their faith and obedience to the teachings of Christ. In the midst of all this turmoil, Peter was reminding His fellow brothers and sisters in Christ of their identity and that they were still chosen and not forgotten. Let us take a closer look at what truth these passages of Scripture are trying to communicate to us.

- **Chosen** generation - God has chosen us. We are His and have been adopted into His family (Ephesians 1:4-6) as a sheer act of grace, not by anything we have done. We were chosen to receive salvation through Christ and enjoy fellowship with God forever. The generation that Peter is talking about is comprised of all people who have accepted the call of salvation and find their identity in Christ Jesus.
- **Royal** priesthood - Before Christ died, the high priest was the only person who could go into the presence of God. Jesus' death and resurrection made Him the supreme High Priest, and our faith in Him gives us the ability to boldly approach His throne of grace (Hebrews 4:16). We are

co-heirs with Christ (Romans 8:17) and have immediate access to the Lord, which also gives us the honor and responsibility to intercede in prayer for others.
- **Holy** nation - We are a part of a unified group of people who have been set apart by God for His service. The Holy Spirit within us is transforming our lives and giving us the ability to walk in holiness. He declared us holy because He is holy (1 Peter 1:16), and we have the unique privilege of sharing in His character because we are His.
- **His own** special people - We are God's possession and His inheritance. By believing in Christ for salvation and having our hearts regenerated by the Holy Spirt, we are given the "right to be called children of God" (John 1:12). Our adoption into His family (Ephesians 1:5) means that God will protect us and complete His good work within us (Philippians 1:6). Our lives do not belong to us (1 Corinthians 6:19-20), and we can look forward to spending eternity by His side (John 10:28).

First Peter 2:9 is about more than just simply knowing our identity in God; we are also called to do something. We are called to make His name known to the world and proclaim His praises to others. You cannot come into the kingdom of God and remain silent. You have an obligation to walk in His light and help bring those who are trapped in darkness to experience that very same light.

We live in a society that tells us we are worth something once we achieve perfection, but God says otherwise. The world accepts us once we achieve perfection, but the Lord accepts us as we are and then makes us perfect in Him. Social media has created a platform for us to share our lives with others at the click of a button. It is a wonderful tool that we can use to network, promote, and communicate with others who are near and far from us. However, there is a downside to this technology. There is a whole generation growing up basing their value, identity, and worth in how many followers, likes, and comments they get on a single picture.

Instead of embracing our differences, it can become easy to compare our lives based on the images that we see as we scroll through our news feed. Social media has become an alternate reality for some people. It has become a place where they can portray the lives they wish they had rather than reflect the truth about their actual lives. We have the freedom to tell the world whatever story we want using filters, apps, and Photoshop in order to post the best images we possibly can. This has become the new normal.

What happens when the reality that you live on social media does not match up with the reality that you face every day? What happens when the reality that you have portrayed on social media doesn't match the person whom people meet in real life?

You end up living a double life.

A whole generation of people is learning that it is okay to be one way on Sunday and live a whole different life on social media the rest of the week. A whole generation is growing up believing that social media is more important than reality. It has become the norm to post whatever we want on social media without thinking about the consequences that our words or actions may have on others. As we sit behind screens all day, there is not a real sense of accountability for our behavior. There is a common misconception that all of our technological advancements and access to multiple social networks will lead to happier lives, but nothing could be further from the truth. A recent study[ix] found the following about Facebook users:

"Insecure people use Facebook more, science confirms." [x]

The researchers who authored this study at Union College in New York discovered that people who felt more insecure in their relationships were among those who spent the most time interacting on Facebook. They tended to post status updates, write on walls, comment on posts and photos, and "like" status updates all in the hopes of receiving a little attention. This attention helped the individual feel more secure in their relationships with friends and family, as well as validated their acceptance and value with others. Now, I am not saying that Facebook or other social media sites, like Instagram or Twitter, are making us insecure, but I do believe that it is highlighting and feeding our insecurities. Our culture is creating pressure for us to be something that we aren't, all in favor of likes and comments. As we scroll down our news feed on our favorite social media platform, comparing and contrasting our lives with others, it is all too easy to forget in Whom our identity lies.

We live in a world where a person's image is super important. We take selfies and use filters to blot out our imperfections instead of embracing the bone structure, body shape, and facial features that He created us with. When God formed us in the womb, He took a step back and said, "It is good," but society has trained us to think that He somehow made a mistake if we don't look like the models during New York Fashion Week or the celebrities on the cover of *GQ*, *Cosmopolitan*, *Essence*, and *Ebony* magazines. We spend countless dollars trying to nip, tuck, and hide our features instead of embracing who we are.

Our society has trained us to believe that the more airbrushed and photoshopped we look, the better. According to the American Society of Plastic Surgeons (ASPS), $16 billion was spent on plastic surgery in 2016 alone.[xi] I don't know about you, but that number was staggering to me. To think that we are putting that much money into our physical appearances instead of embracing who God created us to be is alarming and very disturbing.

While writing this book, I took a two-month break from Instagram and Facebook for a few reasons.

1. To focus and dedicate more time to the completion of this book.
2. To clear and renew my mind.
3. To gain strength and a renewed vision for what God was asking of me without being concerned about what everyone else was doing.

This was so critical for me because there are times when I judge myself and what God has called me to say and do based on the responses I receive on the statements, questions, or images that I post. There are times when I start to question if I'm in the will of God because of what I see on social media.

"WHO DOES GOD SAY I AM?"

With so many people's highlight reels sliding across my screen, it can be hard to remain rooted in Christ. I have to constantly remind myself that who I am is not based on anything or anyone except Jesus Christ. I am not who people say I am; I am who God says I am. It's His approval that I should be constantly seeking, not man's. When I find myself questioning my identity or worth, I go back to Scriptures like Jeremiah 1:5 (NASB) which says,

> *"Before I formed you in the womb I knew you, And before you were born I consecrated you; I have appointed you a prophet to the nations."*

God has known us since before the beginning. We were already chosen to be set apart and to fulfill a call on our lives. The Lord created us to be unique individuals who will use our lives to point people back to Him. There is a reason why He gave us the parents we have. There is a reason why we grew up in the neighborhood we did. There is a reason why we were born in the country we were born in. There is a reason why we have the siblings that we have. God created you to have influence over a particular group of people. You were created to reach someone who I personally may never be able to reach. God's sovereignty extends to the minute details of our lives, and your story is yours for a reason.

If you don't get anything else from this chapter, I want you to understand that as children of God, we don't have to look to temporal things and people to give us our worth or identity. You are valuable not because of your social media followers, relationship status, gender, talents, skin color, bank account, or designer labels. You are valuable because you are created in His image. Everything that God says about us cancels out any label that society attempts to place on us or any lie that the Enemy uses to deceive us. In fact, the next time the Enemy starts telling you that you have no worth or value, remind him:

> *"But you are a **chosen** generation, a **royal** priesthood, a **holy** nation, **His own** special people, that you may proclaim the praises of Him who called you out of darkness into His marvelous light."*
> *1 Peter 2:9 NKJV, emphasis mine*

I truly believe that, in order for us to fully walk in our identity, we must study and meditate on God's Word. When Jesus was tempted by the Enemy in the wilderness in Luke 4, Jesus used the Word of God to overcome Satan. Whether our enemy reveals itself in the form of society, culture, our environment, self-sabotage, or the Enemy of our souls, we can combat those schemes with the truth of Scripture.

Here are 30 different truths that speak to who we are in Christ. I encourage you to meditate on these passages and commit them to memory.

1. New (2 Corinthians 5:17)
2. A Child of God (1 John 3:11, 2 Corinthians 6:18, John 1:12)
3. Chosen (Ephesians 1:4, 1 Peter 2:9)
4. Image Bearers of God (Genesis 1:27)
5. Forgiven (Colossians 2:13, 1 Peter 2:24)
6. Washed Clean (Isaiah 1:18)
7. Beloved (Jeremiah 31:3)
8. Delighted In (Zephaniah 3:17)

9. Free (Galatians 5:1, John 8:36)
10. A Temple of the Holy Spirit (1 Corinthians 6:19)
11. Adopted into God's Family (Romans 8:15, Ephesians 1:5)
12. Co-Heir with Christ (Romans 8:17)
13. Set Apart (1 Peter 2:9)
14. A Co-Laborer (1 Corinthians 3:9)
15. Wise and Restored (1 Corinthians 1:30)
16. His Masterpiece (Ephesians 2:10)
17. Loved (1 Thessalonians 1:4)
18. Wonderfully and Fearfully Made (Psalm 139:14)
19. Victorious (1 Corinthians 15:57)
20. An Ambassador for Christ (2 Corinthians 5:20)
21. Royal Priesthood (1 Peter 2:9)
22. Seated in the Heavenly Places (Ephesians 2:6)
23. Alive in Christ (Ephesians 2:5, Romans 6:11)
24. Overcomer (1 John 5:4-5)
25. More Than A Conqueror (Romans 8:37)
26. Friend of God (John 15:15)
27. Redeemed (Isaiah 43:1)
28. Anointed (2 Corinthians 1:21-22)
29. Free from Condemnation (Romans 8:1)
30. Never Alone (Hebrews 15:3)

Time to Reflect

1. What lies about your identity have you believed?
2. What truth do you need to meditate on this week?
3. Pick two or three verses of Scripture from the list above that will help you combat the lies you have believed.
4. Spend time meditating and reflecting on who God says you are in Him for the next 21 days.

"If then you were raised with Christ, seek those which are above, where Christ is, sitting at the right hand of the God. Set your mind on things above, not on things on the earth. For you died, and **your life is hidden with Christ in God***."*
Colossians 3:1-3 NKJV, emphasis mine

"Therefore, come out from among unbelievers, and separate yourselves from them, says the Lord. Don't touch their filthy things, and I will welcome you. And I will be your Father, and you will be my sons and daughters, says the Lord Almighty."
2 Corinthians 6:17-18 NLT

5

DEATH TO THE COOKIE CUTTER CHRISTIAN

"God has given each of you a gift from his great variety of spiritual gifts. Use them well to serve one another."
1 Peter 4:10 NLT

Over the past few years, the Lord has been opening my eyes to how, within our "Church culture," many of us, including myself, have been deceived by this idea of needing to "fit in." For clarity in this chapter when I use "Church" I am referring to the universal body of believers, but when I use "church" I am referring to the local gatherings of believers. We get so caught up in what we think a Christian should look like or how they should act, that we totally miss out on being the unique and different individuals that He has called us to be. Maybe you don't always feel comfortable being yourself because you fear what others have to say about you. Or maybe you attend a local church where there are a bunch of rules and regulations that you have to follow in order to be accepted and considered a "good Christian." Even though our main purpose in life is to glorify God, we do not all have to be, look, act, speak, write, sing, dress, or worship the same way in order to do so.

There's no place in the Bible that says God called us all to be the same. He has designed us with gifts, talents, and personalities that differ from our neighbors for a reason. When you come to Christ, you don't have to change your personality and become someone God did not create you to be. In fact, when we follow Jesus, we actually discover our truest self as He begins to reveal to us who we were designed to be. As I mentioned before, He can and wants to use your differences to reach a particular group of people, in a particular part of the world, for a particular amount of time. The Lord created you the way you are for a reason. Once you begin to submit yourself to Him, that's when He can actually channel your personality quirks, strengths, and weaknesses to work it out for your good and the good of others to bring Him glory. We actually belittle God's handiwork when we seek to change His original design in an attempt to fit some man-made "Christian ideal."

I remember being in a prayer meeting a few years ago with some of the women at the local church I attended in Atlanta, Georgia. We had gathered to pray and worship before our monthly women's ministry meeting, which I was leading at the time. As I sat on the couch listening to the words of Shaina Wilson's song, "Press in Your Presence," I struggled to focus on the Lord. Instead of tuning into Him, I was distracted by how some of the other women in the room seemed to be full of such reckless abandonment to our King. Here, I was supposed to be leading this group, yet I felt completely inadequate. Some of these women were older than me and had been following God faithfully for years. I could tell by the way they freely worshipped Him that they knew Him intimately. When they prayed, I felt like the walls of Jericho fell down all over again. In that moment of comparison and weakness, I sensed the Holy Spirit pressing these words from God upon my heart:

This is not a competition. I have made all of my children different and unique for a reason. This is not the time for comparison but full surrender to Me. It doesn't matter how one worships or prays to Me. It doesn't matter whether they dance, sing, or cry. I see it all. I hear it all, and I accept and love it all. Don't worry about what others think or say. Stay focused on running your race and staying close to Me, the Author and Perfecter of your faith.

I felt immediate peace, closed my eyes, and worshipped my Savior the best way I knew how. I had been so focused on comparing myself to the other women in the room that I was missing out on an authentic moment with my Heavenly Father. I know now that God was trying to help me break outside of the box that others—as well as myself—had put me into. He wanted to make me comfortable with the way he created me to worship. He wanted to make comfortable with the way He created me to lead. He wanted to make me comfortable with the way I was created to teach. This ended up being a huge lesson for me that year and something that I am continually reminding myself of. It's crazy how easy it is to fall into the trap of feeling like we need to meet a certain standard in order for God to use us!

At times, I struggle greatly with feeling like my life should be a certain way in order for God to work through me. Even while writing this book, I had to constantly pray and ask the Lord to rid me of any unrealistic expectations and comparisons to other writers that I look up to. I do not have to write like anyone else in order for God's message to go forth and be a blessing; I just have to be faithful to do what He says to do. The Lord continues to show me that He wants to use my weaknesses as well as my strengths to bring glory to His name, and the same goes for you. He wants to use the good, bad, and ugly of your life to point people to Him. The Lord doesn't need your perfection; He just needs an available and surrendered heart.

We give God a chance to put His strength on display when we allow Him to work through our weaknesses. None of us is perfect, and when we accept that truth, God is glorified even more through our lives! I make mistakes and fall short of God's glorious standard every single day, but His mercy, grace, and forgiveness cleanses me and keeps me from being a slave to those mistakes.

I stumbled across this quote a few years back that I use to this very day to help me check the motives of my heart.

"Our desire to be polished and perfect is often proof of a desire for personal glory, not God's glory."
- Michele Cushatt (Propel Women)

Reread that a few times.

God doesn't need us to be perfect in order to get glory through our lives, so why do so many of us choose not to be open and transparent about our Christian walks? Why do so many of us brand ourselves on social media as being poster children for Christianity? Why do so many of us lie when people ask how we are doing? Why do so many of us suffer in silence and isolate ourselves when we are feeling weak and vulnerable? So many people are turned off by Christianity because they feel like it's a religion that requires people to be perfect or inauthentic. And it's no wonder they feel that way because that's what we, as Christians, at times, portray. I cannot even count the number of times I have asked a Christian how they were doing, and they responded by saying, "I'm blessed and highly favored," when I knew they were going through a rough time. It's that exact type of response that can be a turn off for some who don't share our faith in Jesus.

While God has called us to believe the best and remain steadfast in His truth, this doesn't mean that we can't share our trials, shortcomings, and even joys with others. Maybe we have a hard time being transparent about our struggles and weaknesses because we think God can't use our imperfections. Or maybe we are ashamed to admit that we actually don't have it all together as we desire. Just maybe we are too concerned with maintaining the image that we want people to think reflects our lives. No matter the reasoning, don't believe the lies of Satan or our culture that life is about attaining some unrealistic level of perfection. Life is about being obedient to God and being open to His work in our lives. Now, I recognize that, for some, it has less to do with maintaining an ideal of image of perfection and instead, has more to do with trust issues based on past experiences, which makes us more cautious about whom we share our business with.

While I believe there is wisdom in that, we are not called to live in isolation. We all need people with whom we can openly share our lives. If you do not have people in your life that you feel comfortable sharing your sins and wins with, then pray that God would send those types of individuals into your life. He wants to use the local church to help heal you from the hurt and pain you may have experienced in your past.

If you study the New Testament books of Matthew, Mark, Luke, and John, you will find that when Jesus chose the disciples, He didn't go for those who had it all together. He chose those whom some would refer to as teenage rejects and misfits. Jesus didn't go to the temple to find the brightest scholars of the time. He went looking for fishermen and a tax collector. If Jesus were alive today, that would be the equivalent of Him going to the inner-city street corners of Dallas to choose His men and bypassing all of the people enrolled in seminary. The disciples weren't perfect before or after He chose them. What set them apart from everyone else was their willingness to follow, obey, and let Jesus use them—in all their imperfections—for the purpose of His glory.

Our problem is that many of us are striving to be so perfect that we are leaving the perfect God out of the equation. God doesn't require us to be perfect, but instead, desires us to surrender ourselves to Him so that His perfect way may be fulfilled within and through us. There is no such thing as a "perfect Christian." The sooner we stop trying to attach the world's idea of perfection to our Christian faith, the better. We should be striving for excellence—not perfection—in all that we do. God doesn't ask us to be polished and poised at all times; instead, he desires for us to focus on our heart's posture towards Him and to be real about where we are in life with Him and others around us. Truth be told, when we present ourselves as polished and perfect, we become unrelatable to the vast majority of people whom God has called us to reach. We've got to stop putting up a front and pretending that everything is perfect when it's not because it is actually hurting our witness more than it is helping.

If you take a scroll through the Scriptures, you will see people from many different backgrounds with many different strengths and struggles. Just one look at Jesus' closest followers, the disciples, and you will see exactly what I mean. Simon Peter often spoke without thinking and was brash and impulsive. In my mind, I imagine him as this super radical, adventurous, and impulsive type of person. I mean, the guy cut off a man's ear (John 18:10) and was brave enough to walk on water in a storm for goodness sake (Matthew 14:28-29)! And then there's John. He was very ambitious and sometimes judgmental. He, (along with James) wanted to call down fire from heaven on a Samaritan village because they didn't welcome Jesus (Luke 9:53-54)!

But despite their flaws and differences, God still used to do great works in His Kingdom. Jesus ended up using Peter as "the rock" upon which He built His Church (Matthew 16:18), and He appointed John to take care of His mother, Mary, after His death (John 19:26-27). Both men also wrote letters that are now a part of the New Testament in the Bible. Peter wrote 1 and 2 Peter, while John wrote the Gospel of John, 1, 2, and 3rd John, and Revelation.

We all have a special function in the body of Christ, and all of us are needed. Many people view church as a building that they attend on Sundays for service, but in reality, Jesus has called us (His followers) to be the church. The people of God are the *ekklesia*, which is a Greek word that simply means "a called-out assembly or congregation." We have been called out by God to serve others both in organized assemblies and in our day-to-day lives. The church cannot function properly if we are not faithful to serve in the role for which God has purposed for us in that season. The Apostle Paul affirms this truth in his letter to the Romans:

"Just as our bodies have many parts and each part has a special function, so it is with Christ's body. We are many parts of one body, and we all belong to each other. In his grace, God has given us different gifts for doing certain things well. So if God has given you the ability to prophesy, speak out with as much faith as God has given you. If your gift is serving others, serve them well. If you are a teacher, teach well. If your gift is to encourage others, be encouraging. If it is giving, give generously. If God has given you leadership ability, take the responsibility seriously. And if you have a gift for showing kindness to others, do it gladly."
Romans 12:4-8 NLT

According to this passage, every believer has a gift that was given to them by God, and we are all called to use our gifts to support and build up the Body of Christ. We don't get to pick the gifts we receive, but we are required to use them to serve one another. Another thing to note is that we aren't called to do everything, but we are called to do something. Different seasons of life may require us to serve and use our gifts and talents in different ways, but at the end of the day we are still called to use them for the benefit of others in a local church. Maybe you are someone who is more of a visionary with a strong desire to shepherd others, and God has called you to be a leader of an organization. Or maybe you are very organized and have the gift of administration that will assist the leader in fulfilling the vision. Maybe God has called you to be behind the scenes baking and cooking for the homeless while another has been called to lead worship in front of the congregation. Each one of you is needed, has value in the Body, and has been called by Christ to do His good work. In fact, God has wired you the way He has in order for you to serve in the way that He has intended for you to serve. Your life story, background, and history has ultimately prepared you to share the light of Christ with a particular group of people. Our Heavenly Father, in His grace, has equipped you with gifts and empowered you to reach those within your sphere of influence. What does this mean for us? You don't need to adopt someone else's mannerisms, talk the same way that your pastor does, or pray the way that your grandmother does in order to be effective in ministering to others. All you have to do is function in your giftedness, while submitting to Christ, and you will see just how God is able to move in and through you to impact the world around you, for His glory.

> *"The human body has many parts, but the many parts make up one whole body. So it is with the body of Christ. Some of us are Jews, some are Gentiles, some are slaves, and some are free. But we have all been baptized into one body by one Spirit, and we all share the same Spirit*

Yes, the body has many different parts, not just one part. If the foot says, 'I am not a part of the body because I am not a hand,' that does not make it any less a part of the body. And if the ear says, 'I am not part of the body because I am not an eye,' would that make it any less a part of the body? If the whole body were an eye, how would you hear? Or if your whole body were an ear, how would you smell anything? But our bodies have many parts, and God has put each part just where he wants it. How strange a body would be if it had only one part! Yes, there are many parts, but only one body. The eye can never say to the hand, 'I don't need you.' The head can't say to the feet, 'I don't need you.' In fact, some parts of the body that seem weakest and least important are actually the most necessary. And the parts we regard as less honorable are those we clothe with the greatest care. So we carefully protect those parts that should not be seen, while the more honorable parts do not require this special care. So God has put the body together such that extra honor and care are given to those parts that have less dignity. This makes for harmony among the members, so that all the members care for each other. If one part suffers, all the parts suffer with it, and if one part is honored, all the parts are glad. All of you together are Christ's body, and each of you is a part of it."
1 Corinthians 12:12-27 NLT

Every member in the Body of Christ has value, worth, and dignity. The person who serves as an administrative assistant is just as important as the youth Bible study teacher. The person who runs the soup kitchen is just as important as the associate pastor. The person who greets people at the front door is just as important as the worship pastor. Until we recognize the inherit value of each member and the need for each other, we will not thrive or be truly effective in expanding God's Kingdom. Everyone can't be the same because God didn't create us to be the same. In order to advance the cause of Christ, we must be free to operate in different areas of service. The Lord is not asking us to walk in uniformity but is asking us to walk in unity as we reach the lost and build up His Kingdom. No matter what our role is in the Body of Christ, we can be confident that God has gifted us to support others and bring glory to His name. It is up to us to be good stewards of whatever God has gifted us with and to stay humble in the process.

If I could sum this chapter up in four sentences, it would be this:

FOLLOW CHRIST.
BE YOU.
BE AUTHENTIC.
LEAD OTHERS TO CHRIST.

I will be the first to tell you that this is not always an easy process. Sometimes, it is a lot easier to just "fit in" with the crowd—even amongst other believers. We must aim daily to be the women and men whom God desires for us to be regardless of how uncomfortable that makes other people feel. There is a purpose for and a calling on our lives that we cannot not make any apologies for. When we submit to Christ, follow His path, stay true to who He has created us to be, and are genuine, people will take notice, and doors will be opened for us to share our faith. Let us all shine bright and be the light that He has called us all to be in this dark world! He loves us enough to make us different so that we can support and encourage one another in fulfilling His Kingdom work. It's not about us. It always has been and always will be about Him.

Time to Reflect
1. In what ways have you felt pressured to conform to a perfect or particular "Christian image" in the church?
2. How will you move forward in being transparent with others about where you are in life?
3. In this chapter, we discovered the importance of recognizing the value of your service in the church in order to build up the Kingdom of God. In what ways will you serve in your local church?

> *"He makes the whole body fit together perfectly. As each part does its own special work, it helps the other parts grow, so that the whole body is healthy and growing and full of love."*
> *Ephesians 4:16 NLT*

Part 3

THE PROCESS

Journaling from My Heart: No Condemnation

October 17, 2017

Today was one of those days where I had to remind myself that I can't earn God's love by my "good behavior." He loved me even when I was still a sinner and His enemy (Romans 5:8-11), so now that I'm His child, there is no condemnation (Romans 8:1). My good works are the evidence of my faith, but they don't save me. It's by His grace that I am saved through faith (Ephesians 2:8), and it's His grace that keeps me. So, I don't have to perform and put on a show for Him, and when I fall short, He's right there waiting to forgive, cleanse, and restore me. Does that mean I abuse His grace by continuing to sin (Romans 6:1)? No! His grace actually empowers me to do what pleases Him! It just means that I don't have to walk around with unnecessary guilt and shame when I do sin because Jesus paid my debt at the Cross!

This isn't a since-I'm-loved-by-God-unconditionally-I-can-do-whatever-I-want type of deal. It's a God-loves-me-in-spite-of-myself-that-I-want-to-serve-you-forever type of deal. When I make a mistake, You aren't shaking your fist at me from heaven. Instead, You are calling me to repentance and back into the sweet fellowship that Christ died on the Cross for. Someone once told me, "There's nothing you can do to cause Him to love you any more than He does right now. There's nothing you can do to cause Him to love you any less right now either." It took me a while to believe that, but here I am, years later, able to walk in that truth, and you know what; it makes me want to obey and fellowship with You, Lord, even more.

# 6

SET FREE

"Therefore, if the Son makes you free, you shall be free indeed."
John 8:36 NKJV

Our past experiences tend to shape how we view our current world. Those who have not had the privilege of growing up in a two-parent household will not have the same experience as someone who has. A child who was molested at a young age will not grow up the same as one who has not experienced such trauma. Though our life experiences may be different, all of us carry baggage and have issues to deal with. Even people who grew up in the most loving, godly, and Christian homes have made mistakes in the past, experienced trauma, and have patterns of sin to overcome. Thankfully, though, when we come to Christ, we are given a second chance and become new creatures in Him. We are no longer bound by our past and the sins that we have committed or that were committed against us. God declares us in right standing (righteous) with Him, and we are justified by our faith in Christ's sacrifice for our sins. That truth is what has freed me and continues to free me from the hurt, pain, and rejection that I have encountered in my life. I'm grateful that Jesus' death means that I don't have to live enslaved to the mistakes of my past any longer.

I spent so much of my early Christian life in the bondage of mediocrity. I practiced all of the religious activity, but my life was powerless. I was not living a life that would cause an unbeliever to take notice and want to follow God. I lived with so much fear, had no fight, and had no true understanding of what it meant for me to have been bought with a price. I had no idea that I could walk with authority and power over the Devil. For many years, I battled with low self-esteem, people pleasing, feeling the need to lower my standards for others, fear, basing my worth off others' compliments or critiques, and a lack of confidence in my abilities. As I write this, there are still some days in which some of these things seek to plague my heart and mind. The difference is that, these days, I do my best to fight back with truth because I know *Whose I am*, and that has given me the ability to walk in victory instead of defeat. There is a clear difference between fighting to walk in liberty and voluntarily giving in to defeat. Some days are harder than others, but the Lord promises to never leave nor forsake us (Deuteronomy 31:6).

Let me be the first to tell you that this journey of being set free doesn't always happen instantaneously or overnight. Depending on the trauma of your past or what your stronghold is, it might take time to experience complete and total freedom, but you can start today by declaring that victory is yours by the power of the blood of Jesus. The Devil wants us to believe that because we still struggle or experience temptation in certain areas, we aren't really children of God or that God doesn't hear our cries, but we must remember the Devil is a liar (John 8:44). It is not a sin to be tempted; rather, it's how we choose to respond to the temptation that results in us either turning away from (walking by the flesh) or drawing near to God (walking by the Spirit). Our God is faithful, and as long as we keep seeking Him, we will experience victory as His children.

We can be sure of this fact: God wants us to walk in freedom. He sent His son to die on the cross so that you and I could be free from the bondage of sin. Jesus rose on the third day to show us that He has the power to overcome anything, even death. His resurrection is proof that we, too, can be freed from even the worst sins, circumstances, and scenarios. From the beginning—even before the book of Genesis—the Lord had a plan to one day offer us a way to be men and women who served, lived, worshipped, loved, and worked from a place of freedom. And the best thing about this freedom is that it costs us nothing, and it cannot be taken away from us. This freedom is only available in and through Christ, and we have to make a conscious decision to operate in it. When we don't walk in that freedom, we miss out on experiencing the fullness of what it means to be a child of God.

I am a big history person. I absolutely love watching documentaries and going to museums to learn more about the stories of those who have come before me. Growing up as a homeschooler, I had the unique experience of my mom making history come to life for me. We would travel on vacation just to see the places that we were studying in our history textbooks, and I often imagined what it would have been like for me to live in certain periods throughout history.

Just recently, I was researching African-American slavery in the United States. I found out that, when the Emancipation Proclamation, the document that declared of all the slaves free, was issued by Abraham Lincoln on January 1, 1863, the slaves in Texas didn't hear about the news for another two and a half years on June 19, 1865. This meant that, although they were legally free, they were still actually functioning as slaves. And even after they were granted their freedom, some of the slaves just stayed and worked on the same plantations because it was all that they knew. Actually walking out their freedom meant taking a risk and stepping into an unknown world that didn't offer them much support or opportunities for work. It meant being uncomfortable in an unfamiliar environment.

As I look around today, unfortunately, I see many Christians living out a similar scenario, myself included. Many of us are either unaware of the freedom that Christ has purchased for us, or we don't walk in that freedom on a daily basis. Why are Christians still sitting in jail cells of sin when Christ has opened the door and invited them to come out? Oftentimes, I think it has a lot to do with our unbelief. It's easy for us to go through the routine of practicing religion without it having a real impact on our lives. Yes, we can recite Scripture. Yes, we attend church on Sundays. Yes, we pray before our meals. But generally, that is where we stop. We miss out on going deeper and experiencing the true freedom that was bought for us because we settle for a Westernized version of Christianity that is safe and comfortable.

In the first few chapters of this book, we focused on discovering what God did for us and who He has called us to be. Next, on our journey of discovering the unfailing and unconditional love of God, we must begin to understand that we have been set free. His unconditional love prompted Him to make a way for us to be free from all condemnation. We are free from the bondage of sin, death, and anything else that does not stem from righteousness. We no longer have to be controlled by the lusts of the flesh, but sadly, many Christians today do not live in this truth. Instead, we live very defeated lives and forfeit the victory that was already won for us at Calvary. Jesus came to set the captives free! We were the captives, but thanks be to our Lord and Savior Jesus Christ who sacrificed His life so you and I could experience life abundantly; we are free!

> *Being free allows us to approach God in confidence.*
> *Being free allows us to love others.*
> *Being free allows us to forgive others.*
> *Being free allows us to live out God's calling on our lives.*

Scripture gives us many examples of this truth.

> *"Because of Christ and our faith in him, we can now come boldly and confidently into God's presence."*
> *Ephesians 3:12* NLT

"For you were called to freedom, brothers. Only do not use your freedom as an opportunity for the flesh, but through love serve one another."
Galatians 5:13 ESV

"Bearing with one another and, if one has a complaint against another, forgiving each other; as the Lord has forgiven you, so you also must forgive."
Colossians 3:13 ESV

"Therefore, let it be known to you, brethren, that through Him forgiveness of sins is proclaimed to you, and through Him everyone who believes is freed from all things, from which you could not be freed through the Law of Moses."
Acts 13:38-39 NASB

"But now you are free from the power of sin and have become slaves of God. Now you do those things that lead to holiness and result in eternal life."
Romans 6:22 NLT

What exactly is bondage? Let's take a closer look. The *Merriam-Webster Dictionary* defines bondage as:

servitude or subjugation to a controlling person or force
a state of being bound usually by compulsion
captivity[xii]

Before Christ, every single one of us was in bondage to sin. We were spiritually dead and hadn't become the new creations that the Lord had designed us to be. The old had not passed away, and the new had not begun. This bondage of sin robs you of the ability to do all that God has called you to do and be all

God has called you to be. It blinds you to the things and ways of God. When we become followers of Jesus, we are freed from that bondage. Reminding ourselves of who we are in Christ is essential to us seeing that freedom demonstrated in our day-to-day lives. We have an adversary who is fighting to keep us from walking in freedom because He knows that when we are bound in our minds, finances, marriages, churches, communities, and homes, then the impact and advancement of God's Kingdom will be limited.

The Holy Spirit gives believers the power to walk in freedom from sin every day. Imagine if we lived in a time when believers didn't have that blessed luxury. In the Old Testament, people had to offer blood sacrifices every single time they sinned against God, and the Holy Spirit only rested on people as God willed for a specific period of time. They did not have access to an indwelling Helper who would empower them daily. It wasn't until Christ became our sacrifice once and for all at Calvary and sent the Holy Spirit that we now we have this unlimited access to life-altering freedom.

> *"For God is working in you, giving you the desire and the power to do what pleases Him."*
> Philippians 2:13 NLT

We can rest assured that, as we pursue the Lord daily, He is doing a work in us. The Holy Spirit not only gives us desires that are in line with what God desires, but He also gives us the power to live them out. We are not left to our own devices; God has set us up for success like the good, good Father that He is! This work is an ongoing process that won't be complete until we receive our glorified bodies in heaven. He knows that, apart from Him, we cannot achieve anything that has true lasting value. We could spend our whole lives trying to better ourselves, but if we aren't relying on the power of the Holy Spirit, our attempts are futile. Oh, how I am glad that God has saved me (justification), is saving me (sanctification), and will continue to save me (glorification)! This is not a one-time ordeal. No, this journey is a process. When we put our faith in Christ, we are spiritually set free, but we are always in the process of continually being set free, and upon His return, we will be finally and fully set free.

None of this meant anything to me until two years ago when I did a personal study through the book of Romans. Through my understanding of justification, sanctification, and glorification, my eyes were opened to the grace, faithfulness, and love of God in a whole new way. Let's take a closer look at these terms to make sure we understand exactly what they mean and how they literally transform the life of every believer:

- **Justification**- The act of being declared righteous (in right standing) by God through a person's faith in Jesus (Romans 5:1, Romans 4:5). Christ's death on the cross grants us access to the only way our sins can be forgiven (John 14:6). Our acknowledgement of this, by faith and repentance, allows our sin debt to be cancelled, and our sins are exchanged for His righteousness. When God sees us, He no longer sees our flaws and shortcomings; instead, He sees the righteousness of His Son (Ephesians 2:13). Christ's sacrifice covers our sins, which causes God to see us as perfect and faultless. Justification brings us into a right relationship with God, grants us peace with Him, and secures our salvation (Romans 5:18-19).

- **Sanctification**- Our daily pursuit of becoming more like Christ and growing in spiritual maturity. Even though our faith in Christ sets us free from the penalty of sin, we don't immediately demonstrate that in our actions, so we must be sanctified (Hebrews 10:14). It is through sanctification that we are constantly being saved from the power of sin. This is an ongoing development in which God teaches us how to live a life that pleases Him as we abide in Him and His Word (John 15:4-5, 7-8). As we abide in Christ, the fruit of the Holy Spirit is produced in our lives, and this brings about holiness so that we can be holy as God is holy (1 Peter 1:15-16). Sanctification is not something that we can do in our own strength, but rather, through the power of the Holy Spirit that works in us as we yield to His guidance in our lives.

- **Glorification**- The ultimate salvation of our whole person, which will occur when we are face-to-face with Jesus in His coming Kingdom. We will be completely like Christ and able to enjoy complete fellowship with God (Romans 8:30, Philippians 3:21). At this point, we will be saved from the very presence of sin and the pain of this world forever and ever.

Why is this good news? Because we do not have to get it all together in one day. It's a constant, steady progression towards Christ-likeness. We can rest in the fact that it is the Lord who has called us to be His children, and He promises to complete the good work in us (Philippians 1:6).

> *"Now the Lord is Spirit, and where the Spirit of the Lord is, there is freedom."*
> 2 Corinthians 3:17 ESV

Although we have been set free positionally, do you ever feel like it is a struggle to feel free? If your life is anything like mine, there are moments when it feels like the dead weights of sin, rejection, pain, and suffering are lingering and cannot be shaken.

I recently held a time of prayer and fellowship with a wonderful group of ladies in my home that was centered around the topic of freedom. These times of prayer are special because they create an opportunity for women of different ages, from different backgrounds, and in different seasons of life to come together to be encouraged, refreshed, and empowered. The question on the table this time was "What does it mean to be free?" and the biggest takeaway was that, although we are free from the power of sin through Christ, we must fight to walk in that freedom on a daily basis. The Enemy loves to steal, kill, and destroy (John 10:10) us with his lies to keep us in bondage, but Christ came "to proclaim liberty to the captives" (Isaiah 61:1). Any condemnation, guilt, fear, or shame that we experience is not from the Lord (Romans 8:1), and He desires for us to "cast our cares" on Him (1 Peter 5:7). Oftentimes, as Christians, we hold ourselves back from experiencing the victory of freedom that has been won for us because we aren't willing to be vulnerable with God and others about what we are dealing with. We are fighting a real Enemy who wants us to believe that we are the only ones who are struggling so that we can be isolated and weak. He will whisper lies of how we are unworthy of forgiveness because of what we did, said, or thought, but we must remind him of what Christ has already done. There is no sin too great that He cannot cover, and His unconditional love welcomes us back to His throne room of grace to obtain the mercy and grace we need (Hebrews 4:16). We serve a Heavenly Father who is gracious, merciful, and kind, and He is eager to forgive, cleanse, redeem, and restore us.

There is such an unexplainable feeling of release and healing that comes when we stop and take time to acknowledge our shortcomings and faults to one another, like James 5:16 instructs us to. The actual issues, pain, or hurt may not immediately go away, but the power of that stronghold is diminished as we seek the face of our Father together, which happened on that Saturday morning. As we sat around confessing our fears, anxieties, sin habits, and worries to one another, there was a beautiful moment in which we realized that not one woman in the room was exempt from having something to share. Every single one of us had baggage that was weighing us down in some way, and the more transparent we were with each other, the "freer" we felt. The atmosphere in the room shifted as burdens were called out and the name of Jesus was called upon. Some of the things we identified as bondage in our lives came from both decisions that we consciously made and things that occurred to us in the past that we had no choice in. As we extended the unconditional love of the Father to one another through the sharing of Scripture, encouragement, and prayer, the feelings of guilt, shame, and bondage were lifted as joy and peace began to flood our hearts. Taking time out to confess our sins and cover each other in prayer reminded us that none of us is perfect and that this Christian journey is more transformative when done in community with other like-minded individuals. Just to clarify, being free is not dependent upon how we feel, but upon our belief in Christ's sacrifice on the cross. We may positionally be set free through Christ (Romans 6:7), but there is a daily process of being set free that involves us actively meditating on Scripture, praying, confessing our sins, and holding each other accountable.

I want you to take a moment and ask the Lord to reveal what you need to be set free from. What are you in bondage to? Whether we want to admit to it or not, we all struggle with something. For some of us, maybe it's our phones or technology. For others, maybe it's food, alcohol, sex, drugs, lying, social media, lust, anxiety, selfishness, or pornography. Your struggle to walk in freedom in those areas does not define who you are, nor does God's love for you cease. In fact, He loves you so much that the Bible says that when we are tempted, He provides a way of escape (1 Corinthians 10:13). Our struggles don't disqualify us from being called His sons and daughters. Instead, when we yield them to God, they qualify us to be examples to others of His power, redemption, grace, mercy, and glory.

I'm not writing to you as if I'm somehow a poster child for this. In fact, quite the opposite is true. There are areas of my life that I am still discovering the need for God's deliverance on a regular basis. The deeper I go in my walk with the Lord, the more I see my need for Him. I need Him to set me free. I need Him to deliver me from myself. I need Him to restore my heart and mind from past mistakes. I need Him to set me free to trust others. I need Him to help me love those difficult people in my life. I need Him to keep me from becoming self-reliant and prideful.

You might be reading this thinking, "I know that I am free in Christ, but how does that apply in my everyday life? It's one thing to grasp a concept of truth, but it's another to actually apply it our lives. What can you and I do on a practical level to walk out this truth found in God's Word?" Let's go back to Philippians 2:13 (AMP),

"For it is [not your strength, but it is] God who is effectively at work in you, both to will and to work [that is, strengthening, energizing, and creating in you the longing and the ability to fulfill your purpose] for His good pleasure."

We must call on the name of the Lord. We must meditate on the Word of God. We must pray and seek His face. We must identify the areas where we are in bondage, ask the Lord to uproot the lies that we have believed, and then replace them with His truth. We must make declarations of faith by speaking God's Word over our lives. We must do our part to get into God's presence and then allow Him to fight our battles. It is His good pleasure to work within us, and when we find ourselves at His feet, we will find that our walk and our talk line up with Him more and more. As we diligently seek Him, we will discover that freedom is not only available; it is attainable. The battle for our freedom is real, but our God fights for us and is undefeated. We are called to fight from a place of victory. We are on the winning team! Many times, we show up to the battle already defeated in our minds with no hope. However, we must realize that we have the victory, and we are the ones who can boldly approach the throne of grace. No matter what we face, we are overcomers through the blood of Jesus Christ.

I went through a brief period in college where I was very judgmental, critical, fearful, and full of pride. I was the embodiment of the expression, "Hurt people, hurt people." When I began to seek the Lord and develop a personal relationship with Him, I realized just how much brokenness affected the way I lived and treated others. Instead of walking in the confidence of being a new creation in Christ, I held onto the baggage of my past. I did not truly understand what being a daughter of God meant, nor did I understand the new life that God was trying to give me. He wanted to exchange His beauty for my ashes. He wanted to exchange his joy for my sorrow. He wanted to exchange His peace for my anxiety. He wanted to exchange His liberty for my captivity. He wanted to exchange His healing for my broken heart.

I remember feeling so free and grateful for this new revelation. I had been hurt and betrayed by so many people throughout my life that it made it hard to trust people. Coming into this new lifestyle, I knew that I needed new friends to help me walk according to the will of God. I got plugged into a local church and was excited to finally be around people whom I could trust. But soon, I found that people in the church are just as broken as people in the world. People who were supposed to be helping me in my healing process were the same ones gossiping about me. I struggled greatly until the Lord reminded me that my hope should be in Him and not in man. What they were saying about me was wrong, but instead of "throwing shade" to them, I was challenged by God to pray for them. As I took the situation to God in prayer, the Lord revealed to me that even in my hurt, He was getting glory. Every time I saw them, my kindness was "heaping burning coals on their heads," as Proverbs 25:21-22 describes. Their words hurt, but it was a driving force to keep me near Jesus in that season. Pretty soon, their words about me no longer had an impact on me because I became more rooted in what God had to say over what man had to say. He used that situation to start the process of delivering me from my people-pleasing tendencies, and today, I am ever so grateful for it. As humans, we are fickle, and our opinions change often, but God and His truth are everlasting.

Last year, I decided to start asking God to give me a word and a Scripture to pray over throughout the year. One of the words that was pressed upon my heart this year is "freedom." I am determined to walk in the freedom that Christ purchased for me. What about you? Will you join me in this journey of exercising our God-given right to live, walk, and serve as free people? Yes, we may live in a society that is not always just, but as children of God, we can be spiritually set free and walk in liberty. Let us not ever forget that Jesus Christ died so that we may have life and the freedom to be the people whom He has called us to be.

Time to Reflect

1. What are some of the things that you need to be set free from?
2. In what areas of your life have you forfeited your freedom as a child of God?
3. What areas of your life do you still need to yield to the Lord?
4. How do you plan to overcome these areas moving forward?

"Then Jesus said to those Jews who believed Him, 'If you abide in My word, you are My disciples indeed. And you shall know the truth, and the truth shall make you free.'"
John 8:31-32 NKJV

"The Spirit of the Lord GOD is upon Me,
Because the LORD has anointed Me
To preach good tidings to the poor;
He has sent Me to heal the brokenhearted,
To proclaim liberty to the captives,
And the opening of the prison to those who are bound."
Isaiah 61:1 NKJV

Journaling from My Heart: Free to Make Mistakes

April 5, 2015

When God designed the plan for your life, it was not dependent on you being perfect. Your mistakes are not a surprise to Him. Sometimes, when I make mistakes, I fall into this trap of thinking that I've somehow ruined God's plan for my life! Thankfully, day by day, He shows me that it isn't true, and I'm learning not to be so hard on myself! God knows everything about us—every sin, every mistake, and every poor decision we have ever made and ever will make—but He still calls us and chooses to use us to advance His kingdom. He loves us in spite of ourselves, and nothing could ever separate us from His love. God does not expect us to be perfect, but He wants us to trust Him, and we can because He is perfect.

We can trust that His grace is sufficient and that His power is made great in our weaknesses. If our hearts and minds are truly set on following Him, we can rest assured that He will honor our obedience and get glory through our lives. There are countless examples of people in the Bible who were not perfect, but God still received glory and honor through their lives. People like David, Noah, Moses, Peter, Sarah, Abraham, and Jonah were all able to be used by God despite their imperfections and mistakes. So, the next time you make a mistake, don't beat yourself up about it. The Lord wants your heart and willingness to obey and live for Him—not a perfect track record!

> "And we know that God causes everything to work together for the good of those who love God and are called according to his purpose for them."
> Romans 8:28 NLT

> "...My grace is all you need. My power works best in weakness..."
> 2 Corinthians 12:9 NLT

7

FINDING SECURITY IN GOD'S GRACE AND LOVE

> *"But God, being [so very] rich in mercy, because of His great and wonderful love with which He loved us, even when we were [spiritually] dead and separated from Him because of our sins, He made us [spiritually] alive together with Christ (for by His grace—His undeserved favor and mercy—you have been saved from God's judgment)."*
> *Ephesians 2:4-5 AMP*

Fear used to be the driving force behind my Christian faith. I felt the desire to please and serve God, but my attempts always seemed to fall short. I viewed God as someone who was ready to inflict punishment on me every time that I made a bad choice. I had no sense of who I was in Christ or what privileges I possessed as His daughter. Despite being a Christian for as long as I can remember, until a few years ago, I served and worshipped the Lord mostly out of obligation rather than a genuine relationship. I went to church and attended Bible studies because that's what I knew to do. I had a surface-level relationship with God and didn't even know it. I was the type of Christian who would pray and call upon Him when I was really in trouble, but when life was going well, I did my own thing. But all of that changed in September of 2012.

I was sitting in my New York City apartment reading a book called *Sacred Singleness* by Leslie Ludy. I had just ended my job as a Resident Chaperone for a summer dance program and was seeking God about what to do next with my life. As I read through the pages of the book, my eyes were opened to the clearest portrayal of the gospel that I had ever heard or seen. It was at that point that I realized I allowed everything and everyone to take God's place in my heart instead of Him. When I thought about Christianity, I thought about rules, regulations, and a long list of "dos and don'ts," but in that moment, I sensed God speaking through this book and beckoning me toward something deeper.

Even though I had grown up in the church as a child, my teenage years were totally different. That strong sense of community and discipleship that were prevalent in my childhood became almost non-existent. Sure, I still had a form of godliness about my life and was a very "moral" person, but I did not have any accountability in place to hold me to Christ's standards. I had grieved the Holy Spirit for so many years that I had almost become completely desensitized to His conviction or leadings. I played the part of a Christian on the outside. I didn't cuss, smoke, or drink, and I definitely wasn't having sex, but the conversations, movies, songs, and books I engaged with were definitely planting seeds of unrighteousness in my life. I was something like the

"Prodigal Daughter." Despite all I had done to grieve the Lord, He never gave up on me. Even though I continually turned my back on Him by choosing the world and its lusts and pleasures, He never stopped pursuing me.

Then, one day, it just clicked for me.

I was at a point in my life where I had been separated from most of my friends, and my dance career was not working out. In my frustration, I grabbed my Bible and a journal. I had been seeing some things on social media about the importance of spending time with God, but my devotional time typically consisted of me saying a 5-minute prayer and going about my day. Today was going to be different. I was going to spend intentional time with the Lord. No distractions, no interruptions—just me, the Lord, and His Word. At first, it was awkward talking to God and pouring my heart out to Him, and honestly, I thought He was going to judge or condemn me. But instead, I encountered His grace and unconditional love, and I grew more and more in love with Him as the days went by. At the time, I worked a few part-time jobs teaching dance in the afternoons, and as soon as my roommates left for the day, I dedicated my entire morning to just sitting at the feet of Jesus. I'll never forget pouring my heart out to God on one of those mornings and sensing the Holy Spirit whispering, *"I've missed you."* He missed me? Where had I been? Then, it hit me like a ton of bricks, and my heart dropped.

As a child, I had considered the Lord my everything, but as I got older, I felt like His commands were too burdensome and old-fashioned. I started to believe preachers just wanted my money in their pockets. I was tired of hearing about having a blessing with my name on it and not seeing any of the evidence. In my eyes, God wasn't interested in my personal life, and I limited Him to the activity during a Sunday service or weekday Bible study. Despite my heart growing colder and my faith diminishing, the Lord remained faithful at attempting to get my attention. Now, here I was at twenty-three years old, and He was showing me that, although I had only let him have access to a tiny part of my life, He had never failed nor forsaken me. I had thought that God was uninterested in the details of my life, but in reality, He had been orchestrating and setting everything up to lead to this present moment.

Growing up as the oldest child in a family definitely presents challenges. When you are your parents' first child, they are so overly cautious with everything because they are new to it and just want to get everything right. My parents were no different, and as a result, I grew up with this idea that making a mistake was a terrible thing. Perfectionism was bred into me as a child and eventually carried over into my relationship with Christ. I spent so much time trying to "earn" God's approval that, when I fell short, I was devastated. I was totally unaware that His grace was sufficient and that He was not asking me to be perfect, but faithful. I praise God now for deliverance from that mindset. A grace-based mindset says that Jesus' finished work on the Cross is sufficient enough to secure our salvation. A works-based mindset says that I must continue to do good deeds in order to secure my salvation. Jesus knew our works would never suffice, which is why He went to the cross on our behalf.

Somewhere in my adult Christian life, I found myself feeling like my actions determined how much God loved me. I lived with this faulty mindset that my "works" earned me a special place in God's heart. It was truly hard for me to understand that God's love for me was unconditional. When life was going well, I assumed that God was pleased with me, and when life was full of trials and trouble, I assumed that God was upset with me. Without a healthy understanding of God's grace, the storms, trials, and tribulations of life can tear us apart. The Enemy will have a field day in our minds stirring up judgment and condemnation. As I mentioned before, He wants to keep us from walking in the authority and freedom that is ours as sons and daughters of God. Once I began to study the Scriptures, the Lord began to open my eyes to see His grace in the right context.

In recent years, I have come to understand the significance of God's sovereignty and the security in His salvation. There is nothing I can do to earn His love, and the Lord doesn't expect me to perform in order to receive His approval. In fact, as I write these words on the page, I need you to understand that I have not arrived. The check list, organized, and planner type of person that I am thrives off of accomplishments and finishing tasks, but God doesn't base his love for me off of my success in life. I must continually preach the gospel to myself in order to be reminded that His love for me is unfailing and steadfast. That is the type of God in whom my salvation lies, and it is secure in His hands. So instead of trying to earn God's love and falling prey to condemnation and guilt every time I make a mistake, I can rest in what Jesus has already accomplished. I am His, and He is mine forever. There are many days when I have to remind myself of this truth by meditating on Scriptures like Romans 8:14-17 (NLT):

> *"For all who are led by the Spirit of God are children of God. So you have not received a spirit that makes you fearful slaves. Instead, you received God's Spirit when he adopted you as his own children. Now we call him, 'Abba, Father.' For his Spirit joins with our spirit to affirm that we are God's children. And since we are his children, we are his heirs. In fact, together with Christ we are heirs of God's glory. But if we are to share his glory, we must also share his suffering."*

Those of us in Christ who have placed our faith in Him alone have the Holy Spirit living inside of us, which is our guarantee that we are His forever. We have the opportunity to approach Him as a loving and kind Father instead of fearful slaves. It wasn't until I came across that passage of Scripture that I really began to be freed from the bondage of seeing God through the lens of the relationship that I had with my earthly dad.

For as long as I can remember, I lived under this feeling of immense guilt every time I made a wrong choice. I would spend hours rethinking through the moment and the harsh criticism of others. This type of thinking left me paralyzed by fear, and I often played it safe. Being the oldest in my family, I felt pressure to set a good example. My parents were quick to discipline us when we made mistakes, and I feared letting them down. Unfortunately, I applied this type of behavior when it came to my relationship with God.

We often view God the same way we view our earthly fathers. In the beginning of my walk with the Lord, it was hard for me to see God as loving, compassionate, and kind because those characteristics were not always demonstrated to me by my own dad. In fact, studies have shown that most of us, whether we realize it or not, have a tendency to view God through the lens of our relationship with our earthly fathers. If we have fathers that are distant or cold in nature, we look at God in that way. If we have fathers who were absent or present but not active in our lives, we tend to expect God to treat us the same way. If we have fathers who gave us our every whim and desire, then we might look to God to do the same. There is a direct correlation between our view of God and our view of our earthly fathers, and many of us need to ask God to heal our hearts and minds in this area. No matter how bad or good your relationship with your father is, God is the perfect Father. He is able and desires to fulfill every longing in our hearts to be accepted, supported, approved of, and loved.

My parents went through a season of difficulties which led to separation for a few years. Those years were hard, and my relationship with my father was super rocky. I lost respect for a lot of men during that period because it seemed as if they were unreliable. For the longest time, I viewed God the same way I viewed my dad. When I succeeded by getting good grades in school, got the lead role in the dance performance, was hired by an employer, or graduated from college, he was quick to applaud. When I made mistakes, it always seemed as if the whole world was about to end. I dreamed of being the little girl whose dad brought her roses at the end of her recitals, but that wasn't my story. I desired a dad whom I could talk to about anything and longed for his affection. I wanted to be understood and heard by my dad in the smallest ways. I have since come to understand that both my dad and mom were doing the best they could do in raising me and my two sisters. In fact, the older I get, I appreciate him more and more for the things that he did and how it opened up doors for God to step in the areas where my dad couldn't. Still, this caused me to struggle greatly in feeling completely accepted by God and being vulnerable with Him in my devotion time. I had to learn not to base who God is on the behavior and words of those around me, but on what He has revealed to us through His Word. I encourage you to ask God to give you eyes to see Him as He is and the capacity to forgive your earthly father by extending grace towards him. As you receive His unmerited forgiveness for your sins, may every wrongdoing of your father be poured out on Jesus at the cross, and may your heart be free to forgive him.

> *"Let all bitterness and wrath and anger and clamor and slander be put away from you, along with all malice. Be kind to one another, tenderhearted, forgiving one another, as God in Christ forgave you."*
> *Ephesians 4:31-32 ESV*

Over the years, I have met people who are unsure of their salvation, and I can totally relate to their fears. Why? I spent years trying to earn God's love because I didn't fully grasp the concept of being eternally secure. I didn't know that once I surrendered my life to Jesus, I was his FOREVER. Nothing could separate me from His love or snatch me out of His grasp. I love the way the Amplified Version of John 10:27 breaks this assurance down for us:

FINDING SECURITY IN GOD'S GRACE AND LOVE

> *"I am the Door; anyone who enters through Me will be saved [and will live forever], and will go in and out [freely], and find pasture (spiritual security). The thief comes only in order to steal and kill and destroy. I came that they may have and enjoy life, and have it in abundance [to the full, till it overflows]."*

Some of us run to the altar and raise our hands every Sunday at church during the invitation for salvation because we don't feel like we are saved. We know that we have sinned in some way and therefore, think we need to get saved again. Let me free you from that mindset right now by telling you this: once you are saved, you are saved. Jesus' blood was shed at Calvary so that you could experience freedom! You don't have to keep putting Him back up on that rugged cross. He died once for all of your sins—past, present, and future. This doesn't give us a license to sin, but it does free us from the condemnation of the Enemy that he loves to throw in our faces. Beloved, when the Enemy taunts you with your sin and tries to condemn you, remind him of what is written in 1 John 1:9 (NKJV):

> *"If we confess our sins, He is faithful and just to forgive us our sins and to cleanse us from all unrighteousness."*

This is one of those moments when we must run to Scripture and stand on the truth. Our salvation is not something that we can gauge off of our emotions because those fluctuate depending on the day. Once you have truly confessed with your mouth and believed in your heart that Jesus Christ is Lord and that He was resurrected, you are His. At that moment, God places the Holy Spirit within you, which proves that you are His.

"Because, if you confess with your mouth that Jesus is Lord and believe in your heart that God raised him from the dead, you will be saved. For with the heart one believes and is justified, and with the mouth, one confesses and is saved. For the Scripture says, 'Everyone who believes in him will not be put to shame.' For there is no distinction between Jew and Greek; for the same Lord is Lord of all, bestowing his riches on all who call on him. For 'everyone who calls on the name of the Lord will be saved.'"
Romans 10:9-13 ESV

"The sheep that are My own hear My voice and listen to Me; I know them, and they follow Me. And I give them eternal life, and they will never, ever [by any means] perish; and no one will ever snatch them out of My hand. My Father, who has given them to Me, is greater and mightier than all; and no one is able to snatch them out of the Father's hand. I and the Father are One [in essence and nature]."
John 10:27-30 AMP

This is the truth upon which we can stand. I suggest that you take some time right now to meditate on that truth. You are His. In fact, you are faithfully His. Our God is able and faithful to keep us. There's not a moment in which He is not thinking about us. The Holy Spirit living on the inside of you is the guarantee that you are a child of God.

Still having trouble grasping this truth? Read Ephesians 1:3-14 (NKJV),

"Blessed be the God and Father of our Lord Jesus Christ, who has blessed us with every spiritual blessing in the heavenly places in Christ, just as He chose us in Him before the foundation of the world, that we should be holy and without blame before Him in love, having predestined us to adoption as

sons by Jesus Christ to Himself, according to the good pleasure of His will, to the praise of the glory of His grace, by which He made us accepted in the Beloved. In Him we have redemption through His blood, the forgiveness of sins, according to the riches of His grace, which He made to abound toward us in all wisdom and prudence, having made known to us the mystery of His will, according to His good pleasure which He purposed in Himself, that in the dispensation of the fullness of the times, He might gather together in one all things in Christ, both which are in heaven and which are on earth—in Him. In Him also we have obtained an inheritance, being predestined according to the purpose of Him who works all things according to the counsel of His will, that we who first trusted in Christ should be to the praise of His glory. In Him you also trusted, after you heard the word of truth, the gospel of your salvation; in whom also, having believed, you were sealed with the Holy Spirit of promise, who is the guarantee of our inheritance until the redemption of the purchased possession, to the praise of His glory."

In this short passage of Scripture, we see that God has chosen us to be adopted into His family. Not only that, He has also blessed us with what we need to do His will, forgave our sins, and sealed us with His Spirit as a promise.

I really wish that someone had broken these Scriptures down sooner in my life because I would have saved myself a lot of insecurity and feelings of hopelessness and abandonment. Once we pass from death into life by believing in the name of Jesus, we are His children, and nothing could ever change that. This is good news. The blood of the precious Lamb was shed once and for all. Jesus only had to die one time to secure our salvation. Oh, how sweet grace truly is!

Time to Reflect
1. What do you think about when you think about God?
2. In what ways has your relationship, or lack of a relationship with your earthly father, affected the way you view God?
3. Are you currently living out a grace-filled or a rules-and-regulation relationship with the Lord?

"Now it is God who establishes and confirms us [in joint fellowship] with you in Christ, and who has anointed us [empowering us with the gifts of the Spirit]. It is He who has also put His seal on us [that is, He has appropriated us and certified us as His] and has given us the [Holy] Spirit in our hearts as a pledge [like a security deposit to guarantee the fulfillment of His promise of eternal life.]"
2 Corinthians 1:21-22 AMP

"For by grace you have been saved through faith, and that not of yourselves; it is the gift of God, not of works, lest anyone should boast."
Ephesians 2:8-9 NKJV

Part 4

ON MISSION

8
CREATED FOR PURPOSE

> *"For by Him all things were created that are in heaven and that are on earth, visible and invisible, whether thrones or dominions or principalities or powers. All things were created through Him and for Him."*
> *Colossians 1:16 NKJV*

You and I have a Kingdom assignment. We were created on purpose for a purpose to bring glory to God.

I'll never forget the day the Lord pressed upon my heart that He had called me to be a writer and speaker. I was standing at the front of my church, in the middle of prayer, when I felt this strong impression from the Holy Spirit, "You will write, speak, and dance for Me." This statement kept flashing through my mind over and over until I finally said, "Okay, God." I was working as a dance teacher in that season, but the Lord was letting me know that my calling was bigger than dance. At that moment, I realized God's plan for my life was going to put me in places that made me uncomfortable but brought Him glory. Our Heavenly Father has a plan and a place for all of us to be light and to proclaim His glory. However, we must be willing to seek Him first and lay aside our selfish ambitions and pursuits.

For 19 years, my life revolved around dance. It meant everything to me, and when I graduated from college, I put all my efforts into becoming a professional dancer. I had gone on many auditions, but there was one audition that would change the course of my life and set me on a path that I never even imagined.

Outside it was dreary and cold, but my spirits were high as I walked into the room where Disney was holding auditions for their cruise line. I quickly glanced around the room as I waited in line to turn in my headshot and resume. It was way less crowded than I'd imagined it would be. This was my third time auditioning for Disney (they say that the third time is the charm, right?), and I just knew that this was what I wanted to do. Not only was the pay decent, but I would also get to travel and finally utilize the passport I had purchased earlier that year.

After turning in my headshot and resume to the Disney representatives, I found a spot in the corner of the room to put my stuff down, put my number on, and prepare myself mentally and physically for what was about to happen. In order to impress the Disney representatives, I needed to be on my A-game. Other dancers sat in groups chatting and stretching, but not me. I reached for my iPod, put on my favorite song, and tuned everyone else out. As I stretched and warmed my body up, I asked God to please allow me to get picked this time.

Suddenly, the door opened, and they called the first group. I gathered my stuff and followed the other dancers into the studio across the hall where the choreographer and casting directors were waiting. This was my chance, and I was determined not to blow it. I was greeted by a familiar face, who happened to be one of the casting directors. He smiled and said, "Good to see you." That little encounter gave me the confidence I needed to dance even better. Forty-five minutes later, they began to dismiss dancers. I was thrilled to make it past all the cuts to the final round. My heart was full of joy as the casting director mentioned that we should be hearing something within the next few weeks about whether or not we earned a spot on the Disney team.

This was it! My dream was coming true. I was finally going to get to walk in my purpose as a professional dancer!

I never did get that email welcoming me into the Disney family. Of course, at the time, I didn't understand why and spent a lot of time being upset that God didn't open a door for me to walk out my dream. Did He truly love me? Did He truly care about my future? Did He want me to starve and not have the provision I needed to pay my bills? I fought back the tears of frustration as these and many other questions flowed through my mind.

Here I was, living in New York City as a recent 2011 Fordham University graduate with a bachelor's of fine arts in dance. I was thrust into the real world and did not have a clue what I would do next. I went from audition to audition, hoping to earn a spot in someone's dance company or even just a small, simple paid gig. However, I rarely ever made any final cuts. The few times I did make it to the end of an audition, I left with high hopes of receiving a phone call or email, but somehow, those notifications never came. I watched as countless classmates joined professional dance companies, danced on television with celebrities, and were asked to be apprentices for up-and-coming choreographers.

I felt lost, confused, and unsure of my future. I had attended one of the most prestigious dance schools in the country and had sacrificed much of my life in training to be a professional dancer. I missed birthday parties, family outings, social gatherings, and even opted out of relationships, just so that I could focus on advancing myself as a dancer. Yet, somehow it seemed like it wasn't enough. There I was in New York City, the dance capital of the world, without two pennies to rub together and a dream that seemed to be dying with each passing second.

I had one desire, and that was to dance and have my name in lights somewhere. I wanted to be able to tell other people that, with hard work and determination, they, too, could make it as a dancer regardless of their skin color. I had faced so many challenges and had overcome so many obstacles during my senior year of college, but nothing prepared me for the devastation of not landing any long-term gigs. I really started questioning who I was and what exactly I was called to do.

Everyone around me had always said to follow my heart and pursue my dreams, but it just wasn't working out the way I had pictured it. I picked up a few jobs, like teaching and assisting dance classes for children so that I could pay the bills, but my heart still wanted to be a part of a company where I could dance full-time. In the dance world, the pay can be little to nothing, and there is often very little stability for freelance artists. I was given a few opportunities to work and travel with a few smaller companies by the grace of God, but they were not consistent enough.

I prayed and cried out to God to give me more opportunities, and often times, it seemed like He was ignoring my cry. Little did I know at the time, it was all a part of His plan to draw me back to Him and set me on a new journey. Dance was the only thing I knew, and it was all I wanted to do, but God knew better.

Dance had consumed my entire life, and my identity had become so wrapped up in it that He couldn't use me the way He desired. At that time, I professed Christ with my lips, but my knowledge of God was limited, and the fruit of my life didn't exactly resemble the fruit of the Holy Spirit. Looking back on that season, I now see that God was closing those doors on purpose, because He wanted to reveal to me the fullness of my true purpose.

I once saw a bumper sticker at a hotel gift shop that said, "We plan, God laughs." That simple quote has stuck with me because many times, we get so wrapped up in what we want that we forget to seek the Lord about what He wants for us. This leads to us spending so much time pursuing a purpose for which we were not created. We try to play God's role and forget that He is Creator and we are His creation.

"A man's heart plans his way, But the LORD directs his steps."
Proverbs 16:9 NKJV

We can make plans for our lives, but ultimately, the Lord is the One who determines the outcome. As His adopted sons and daughters, our lives are not left up to chance. Instead, as we seek the face of our Heavenly Father, He guides us step by step in fulfilling His pre-determined destiny for our lives.

For most of my life, I had believed that my purpose was to dance. I made personal sacrifices for dance, I talked about dance, I read books about dance, I watched videos about dance, I studied dance, and I taught dance classes. Everything in my life revolved around my love and passion for dance. If anything interfered with dance in any way, I immediately eliminated it because of my determination to be a professional dancer and see my name on a billboard in lights. I believed that dancing was all God wanted me to do, and that couldn't have been further from the truth.

He had given me many other gifts and talents that had been overshadowed by the time and energy I spent focused on dance. When He began to reveal that my purpose wasn't to be in a professional dance company, I was devastated, crushed, and felt lost. I couldn't understand why the one thing that I loved so dearly wasn't what God desired me to pursue as a career. Although I had spent nineteen years of my life focused on dance, the Lord was clearly beckoning me on a new journey toward my true purpose and calling. He shifted my focus from myself to living in such a way that His glory was being displayed through my life and gave me a new desire for helping others discover their potential in Christ. As I continued to renew my mind with His Word, I was able to discern that God wasn't calling me to give up dancing; He just wanted to shift the focus of my dancing from entertainment to worship.

Now, I am not saying that it is wrong to pursue a career in dance or any of the other performing and creative art forms. I know plenty of Christians who are using their talents to glorify God in the entertainment industry, but that just wasn't God's plan for me. After a lot of soul-searching, prayer, fasting, and Bible reading, God began to show me that He wanted me to use dance to reach children for Him. He wanted me to spend more time in the studio building relationships and sharing His love with young, aspiring dancers. He wanted me to encourage, support, and build people up in an industry that can be very intimidating and competitive.

All my life, I had an idea of what I thought my life would be like as a professional dancer who would travel the world, but God transformed that idea into something so much better. He had a plan for me to move around, live in different cities and states, mature in my faith, and meet some amazing people along the way. Now, when I look back over my journey, I am so grateful that He did not let me go down the path that I initially planned. Instead of living for myself and my own happiness, I have learned to live out God's purpose in my life and impact as many people as I can for the gospel along the way.

Time to Reflect:
1. In what areas of your life may God be asking you to lay down your dreams and plans in exchange for His?
2. Take a moment to pray and surrender those areas to God. Ask the Lord to align your heart, will, mind, and emotions with His, and to give you a desire for His plan for your life.

FAITHFULLY HIS

"For I know the plans I have for you, declares the Lord, plans for welfare and not for evil, to give you a future and a hope."
Jeremiah 29:11 ESV

9

FULFILLING GOD'S PURPOSE AND MISSION

"For we are His workmanship, created in Christ Jesus for good works, which God prepared beforehand that we should walk in them."
Ephesians 2:10 NKJV

Over the years, I have gotten many emails from individuals, particularly women, with questions and prayer requests about their purpose. Often times, the Lord uses me to redirect them to approach His throne of grace in prayer (Hebrews 4:16) and to seek His Word. Why is that? I believe that we often seek out mankind for answers that God wants to reveal to us. These days, everyone has an idea about what it means to walk in purpose. Some say it means to follow your dreams or your heart. Others say it means to give to the poor and help those in need. It is obvious that even by the world's standards, there is a deep inner desire for us to know why we were born. Just take a trip to your local bookstore or library, and you will see that there are hundreds of books written with the intention of helping people discover their life's purpose. There are thousands of videos on YouTube teaching people how to discover their purpose. There are people charging $100 an hour to help you discover God's plan for your life. While there is nothing wrong with being on a quest for purpose, we must make sure that we are seeking out the right sources when doing so.

Can I let you in on what appears to be a little-known secret? As a believer, your purpose is to honor God, glorify His name, and make disciples of all nations (Don't worry, I won't charge you for that)! The Bible makes this clear in the following passages:

> *"And whatever you do, in word or deed, do all in the name of the Lord Jesus, giving thanks to God the Father through Him."*
> Colossians 3:17 NKJV

> *"Therefore, whether you eat or drink, or whatever you do, do all to the glory of God."*
> 1 Corinthians 10:31 NKJV

> *"Go therefore and make disciples of all the nations, baptizing them in the name of the Father and of the Son and of the Holy Spirit, teaching them to observe all that I have commanded you; and lo, I am with you always, even to the end of the age."*
> Matthew 28:19-20 NKJV

> *"And He said to them, 'Go into all the world and proclaim the gospel to the whole creation.'"*
> Mark 16:15 NKJV

Now, this idea of glorifying God and making disciples definitely plays out in different ways for each of us, but at the end of the day, our ultimate mission in life is to point people back to Him. We are to live our lives in such a way "that they may see your good works and glorify your Father in heaven" (Matthew 5:16). The way you walk out this Kingdom mission may look different in various seasons of life, but the heart of it remains the same. For example, if you are a college student, God may be asking you to serve in a campus ministry and help raise awareness for sex trafficking. If you are a mother of three, maybe God is calling you to focus on discipling your children while your husband works full-time. If you are a teacher, maybe God is calling you to pray over your classroom and share the love of Jesus with all of your students. If you are a widow, maybe God is calling you to pour into young women through a weekly Bible study in your home. If you are a sports coach, maybe God is calling you to shepherd the young girls or boys on your team. All of these examples are different, but they all point back to God and make significant strides toward accomplishing His bigger purpose on the earth of redeeming people by offering reconciliation through His Son Jesus Christ. It's all about pointing people back to Him in our everyday lives and spheres of influence. How you execute God's mission in each season may look different, but at the end of the day, you are called to be a light in the darkness (Philippians 2:15).

There is a difference between calling and purpose. We have already discovered that our purpose in life is to honor God, glorify His name, and make disciples of Jesus, but the *way* we do that is our *calling*. There is no one more qualified in this universe to show you what you are called to do other than God. We must be careful to seek God first rather than run to a bunch of outside sources to help us figure out what or where He is calling us to. It's not wrong to seek wise counsel for direction, but ultimately, He is the only One who knows exactly how He has called us to live out His purpose for our lives. God has given us spiritual leaders for a reason, but if we are not careful, they can become a crutch if we continue to seek them before seeking His throne. In fact, my motto has become "run to the throne of God before you run to the phone."

What are you passionate about? What is the one thing that motivates you to keep pushing? What injustices upset you? These things are not random parts of your personality but rather clues to help you figure out your calling. You and I were crafted in a particular way to serve in particular areas. We can't be anything we want and do anything we want because God created us on purpose to flourish and thrive in what He predestined us to do. Our role is to walk in obedience to what He has already set in motion for us. This doesn't mean that we won't ever work jobs that we aren't completely passionate about, but it does mean that there will still be purpose for us in those places.

Let's say you're a dancer who just got cast into a role for a new Broadway production. On the first day of rehearsals, the choreographer starts by demonstrating the steps that he or she wants you to perform for that particular part. Once the choreography has been given, the group of dancers practices the routine. If you had a question about the choreography, you wouldn't want to ask your fellow dancer; you would go straight to the choreographer because he or she is the one who created the choreography. In the same way, the Lord is the choreographer of our lives, and therefore, He knows the exact steps that we should be taking. As we align our heart, will, mind, and emotions with Him, even the mundane moments of our lives soon become meaningful and full of purpose.

If you seek the Lord, He will show you your calling and your purpose. If anyone ever tries to charge you for it, please run far away. I don't care if they are an apostle, prophet, life coach, or minister—it is not biblical to have to pay money to discover why God designed you. Just simply get alone with God for as long as it takes. This isn't an overnight thing. It takes time and is often revealed to us in pieces as we continue to surrender and submit ourselves to Him. As we go about obeying Him in the small things, the Lord will begin to shape our hearts and reveal to us the plans He has for us. His desires become our desires as we seek to delight ourselves in Him. You can save yourself a lot of money, energy, and time by choosing to sit before God's throne. We cannot let our desire for instant gratification cause us to try to rush God. He will reveal all of the necessary information in due time if we remain faithful to seek Him.

If you are reading this and you're unsure of where to start, I want to recommend that you set aside some time everyday to spend some time with the Lord. This time can include prayer, reading of the Bible, worshipping, Scripture mediation and memorization, and anything else you can think of to help you set your affections towards Him. Developing a daily time with God is truly important because if we don't seek Him, we cannot find out what He is asking of us. If we aren't in the habit of sitting in His presence, it will be harder for us to discern what He is calling us to do and where He is calling us to do it. Having a daily devotion time might mean setting aside 30-60 minutes in the morning before you start your day to renew your mind with His Word. It might mean staying up late after your kids have gone to sleep to listen to a sermon or waking up early to take a prayer walk around your neighborhood. For me personally, I aim to set aside 60-90 minutes in the morning to journal, worship, read my Bible, meditate on Scripture, and/or pray. Some days, I might dance to worship music for most of the time or do an in-depth study on a particular passage of Scripture that the Holy Spirit leads me to. Other days, I might split the time 50/50 between praying and reading a portion of Scripture out of a Bible reading plan. It's less about being able to check it off of your to-do list and more about being intentional and faithful to the time you have set aside. The Lord desires to spend time with us individually in that secret place. It's in that place that He is able to reveal Himself to us in greater ways and bring our desires, dreams, and passions into alignment with what we are called to do. Our intimate time with the Lord prepares us to do the work God has called us to do with the people with whom He has called us to work. We must be filled in that secret place of intimacy with Him if we truly want to be effective in fulfilling God's Kingdom mission. As we are filled with His truth, our hearts and minds are open to be led by Him.

Paul Mints, a minister I once heard speak, put it like this, "Sometimes the revealed will of God must be obeyed before God will show us His specific will."[xiii] Oftentimes, we want God to reveal to us our specific calling, but haven't taken the time to make sure we understand and are following His will as revealed to us in the Scriptures. For example, 1 Thessalonians 5:16-18 (NKJV) tells us to, "**Rejoice** always, **pray** without ceasing, in everything **give thanks**; for *this is the will of God* in Christ Jesus for you" (emphasis mine). Let's be honest: how many of us are actually obedient to this revealed will of God? If we spent more time focusing on obeying passages like this one, where God has clearly outlined His will, our lives would be full of so much more life and purpose. You see, when you obey the revealed will of God and walk in obedience to His Word, the Lord begins to shape and mold your heart to develop passion in particular areas. He opens your eyes to begin to see the world as He sees it, and the needs for justice, faith, peace, love, grace, and hope in the lives of those around you.

When I was growing up, I never would have thought that I would be working in low-income communities in Dallas, Texas. I was focused on becoming a professional dancer, but when I surrendered my will to God and began to walk out His truth, He developed new desires in me that led to new passions. Now, I can't even imagine not working in communities with those who often have been marginalized. I'm grateful that God didn't allow me to pursue my dream but instead gave me new dreams that have allowed me to be like Jesus amongst His image-bearers.

The Lord has gifted you with talents and spiritual gifts for such a time as this (Esther 4:14). He has crafted you fearfully and wonderfully to do something that will reach a specific group of people at this point in history. As we discussed in Chapter 5, we are one body with many parts. We find the greatest fulfillment in life when we use our talents and spiritual gifts to bless others. Our lives are not about us but about serving God and others. I'm not here to tell you what your calling is, but I am here to tell you that you have one, and I encourage you to seek God for it. Your life matters, and He has so much in store for you.

Although I never got to realize my childhood dream as a professional dancer, the Lord has been faithful to grant me opportunities to utilize my passion for dance in other ways. I am so thankful that God loved me enough to redirect my steps towards a different mission, a Kingdom mission. I may never get to put "Disney Cruise Dancer" on my resume, but my name is written in the Lamb's Book of Life. I know that walking in obedience to God far outweighs any human accomplishment or title that I could ever receive here on this earth.

Time to Reflect
1. Have you acknowledged that your main purpose in life is to glorify God and make disciples?
2. How are you using your gifts and talents to glorify God?
3. How could you be a better "light in the darkness" in your workplace, school, community, church, and/or home?

"The counsel of the Lord stands forever, The plans of His heart to all generations."
Psalm 33:11 NKJV

Part 5

RESTING IN GOD'S FAITHFULNESS

Journaling from My Heart: God is Constant

April 18, 2010

Sometimes life gets tough, and it seems like everything is falling apart. My family is fighting, and my finances are in disarray. I am just ready to give up. I turn to those who are close to me, but in the end, no one understands me…no one, that is, except you, Lord. I hear Your sweet voice calling out to remind me that "You will never leave me nor forsake me" (Deuteronomy 31:6).

10

WHAT HAS GOD PROMISED?

"God is not a man, so He does not lie. He is not a human, so He does not change His mind. Has He ever spoken and failed to act? Has He ever promised and not carried it through?"
Numbers 23:19 NLT

According to *The New Oxford American Dictionary* a promise is "a declaration or assurance that one will do a particular thing or that a particular thing will happen."[xiv] The concept of making, keeping, and breaking promises isn't something that is foreign to most of us. Many of us grew up sharing secrets and then asking others to "pinky promise" or swear that they would not tell anyone else.

When I was growing up, I remember asking my parents for things on numerous occasions. I wasn't always sure if they would come through on their end of the bargain, so I would ask them to promise me. If my mom responded by saying "Yes, I promise," then I knew that she was going to do it without a doubt. Her promise meant that I could trust her to come through. In the same way, God lays out promises for us in His Word, and we can trust that He will come through. The Word of God is alive and active, and the God we serve is the same yesterday, today, and forevermore.

On August 22, 2016, I wrote this in my journal:

God ALWAYS delivers that which He has promised!

This was a declaration of faith that I had to continue to speak over myself because in that season, it seemed like my life was crumbling to pieces. I had little to no hope, no money, no job, no permanent place to live, and no idea what to do next. The only thing I could do was stand on the promises of God and wait. It was in that season that I learned what it truly meant to stand still and wait on the Lord.

In the Bible, a promise is the assurance of God to be faithful to His Word. All throughout Scripture, including both the Old and New Testaments, we witness God being faithful to keep the promises He gave to His people. We also witness men walking in rebellion to God and still being on the receiving end of His mercy when they choose to confess their shortcomings and repent of their sin. It's this continuous cycle of a promise made, instructions given, rebellion, judgement, repentance, and mercy that echoes throughout the pages of the Old Testament. Yet, in spite of all of the rebellion of mankind, the Lord has been faithful to keep His promises. This is an act of unconditional love and unfailing compassion towards us that we do not deserve. We deserve to receive the wrath and judgment of God, but because of our faith in Christ, we receive grace, mercy, forgiveness, and access to all of the promises as written in His word.

We serve a God who cannot fail. We never have to worry about Him not coming through on any of His promises. Second Corinthians 1:20 (ESV) says:

> *"For all the promises of God find their Yes in him. That is why it is through him that we utter our Amen to God for his glory."*

When we doubt God, we miss out on entering into His rest. We serve a Father whose desire is to see His children completely trust Him no matter what happens. We aren't supposed to walk in fear, worry, doubt, or anxiety. When I look back over my life and all the various situations I have faced, I noticed that the times when I was most at peace occurred when I was standing on the Word of God and meditating on His truth.

God's heart is to see his children enter into His rest by standing on the promises that He has outlined in His Word. The Bible is full of thousands of promises, but they are only valid for those who have placed their faith alone in Jesus Christ for the remission (forgiveness) of their sins. Some of the things that God promises us, as His children, are healing, salvation, deliverance, provision, faith, joy, hope, and peace, just to name a few. We serve a God who keeps His promises. Now, we may not always agree with the methods that He uses to execute or fulfill those promises, but one thing is for sure: God is not like man, and He cannot lie. His very nature and character are truth, and the Bible is the source through which the Lord has chosen to reveal that to us. The Scriptures show us who God is, what He requires of us, and the benefits we receive for being His people. The Lord has promised to be with us and to equip us for every task, assignment, or mission that He calls us to in addition to the trials and tribulations that come along with it.

"All Scripture is inspired by God and profitable for teaching, for reproof, for correction, for training in righteousness; so that the man of God may be adequate, equipped for every good work."
2 Timothy 3:16-17 NASB

Many of us are not equipped, because we rarely open the Bible. The level of biblical illiteracy is steadily growing year by year. According to a study done in 2017 by Lifeway Research[xv], only 45% of people who attend church regularly read the Bible more than once a week, while about 40% of church-goers read their Bible once or twice or month. This is not due to lack of access because, according to the American Bible Society, 87% of Americans own a Bible, and most church-goers own an average of three.

Now, these statistics were based on church-goers in America, but one doesn't have to do much research to see that this isn't just an American issue. Why do I bring this up? Because many of us are waiting on a move from God, but we do not even know what He requires from us as His people. We want God to fulfill His promises in our lives, but many do not even know what those are or aren't living in a way that would allow us to steward them well. We have access to the source of life itself, but as our Bibles collect dust on a shelf, we begin to look less and less like the Church and more and more like the world.

WHAT HAS GOD PROMISED?

I would guess that 99.9% of you who are reading this right now own some sort of technical device, whether it is a cell phone, laptop, tablet, or MP3 player. Think about how many times a week you charge that device. Most of us are probably charging it at least one time a day, depending on our level of usage, right? If you don't charge it, what will happen? It eventually loses power and dies. The same thing happens to us spiritually when we aren't spending time in God's Word. As the days turn into weeks, that light that Christ put in us begins to diminish, and we lose our saltiness. Matthew 4:4 (NKJV) says, "But he answered and said, 'It is written, Man shall not live by bread alone, but by every word that proceedeth out of the mouth of God.'" We need God's Word in order to live the life that He has called us to live. What if we charged our spirits up with the same fervency that we charge our devices? What if we memorized His Word the same way we memorize the lyrics to our favorite songs? What if we shared the truth within the pages of the Bible the same way we gossip and speculate over our favorite television shows and sports teams?

Part of discovering the unfailing and unconditional love of God means diving into the Scriptures and discovering what He has to say about Himself, the world, and us. Until we become students of God's Word, we will fall for anything. The more you focus on meditating on God's Word, the more confident you become in Him. Good theology is important when we are going through tests, trials, and tribulations because it is often at the sign of trouble that the Enemy tempts us to believe that God isn't good, God doesn't care, or God isn't with us. As we navigate through hardships, the Enemy of our soul works hard to get us to doubt God's sovereignty and love for us in hopes that we would run from God instead of running to Him. When we don't know what God's Word says, we are easy targets for the Devil to steal our faith and confidence in the Lord.

Good theology helps you to remain unshaken when you encounter the storms of life. You may fall, but you get back up because you understand that what God says trumps whatever your feelings or emotions are at the time. The reason why many people turn from God in the hard times is because they have a faulty view of Him. Instead of running to Him, we tend to run from Him out of fear, disappointment, embarrassment, shame, or hurt. The Bible tells us in Psalm 46:1 (NKJV) that He is our "*…Refuge and strength, A very present help in the time of trouble.*" According to *The New Oxford American Dictionary*, the word "refuge" means "a condition of being safe or sheltered from puruit, danger, or trouble."[xvi] This particular word in Hebrew is "ma ·hă ·seh," which means "shelter." It assures us that, whenever we are going through our hard times, God is literally a shelter for us. He is the safety net that we can run to for guidance, strength, support, encouragement, love, and peace. We don't have to run this race alone. We serve a God who meets us where we are. The Lord has chosen us to be His sons and daughters. As I mentioned before, we were literally adopted into His family upon our conversion. He doesn't need us but instead, chooses us because of His love for us. And that love is able to keep and sustain us in every season of life.

The Lord wants us to know what He has promised us and to believe Him. Some of the issues that we have in our lives today have more to do with the fact that we don't know or fully believe what God has promised us rather than the idea that God is not faithful enough to come through. Sometimes I think we forget that God knows us better than we know ourselves. He is omnipresent, omniscient, and omnipotent! He knows that you have bills due; He knows that you need food, gas, or that you need a new job. He created you, and we can rest in the fact that He hears us when we pray and that He will provide it exactly when we need it! We have to learn how to rest and trust in God better when unplanned circumstances arise in our lives, because although they may be a surprise to us, our circumstances never surprise Him. His Word is our anchor and weapon to hold onto in every season of life. We could save ourselves a lot of drama, heartache, stress, and anxiety if we learned to trust God in all circumstances. He makes all things work together in the end for those who walk uprightly!

Now, we must be careful that we don't take Scripture out of context to fit our selfish purposes and desires. The Lord doesn't promise to fulfill all of our desires but does promise to fulfill all of our needs. Our God should not be treated like a genie in a bottle, as we often have a part to play in receiving what God has promised us in His Word. Yes, God is willing and able to fulfill what He has promised, but are you and I willing to be obedient to what He says in His Word? As we delight ourselves in His presence through praying, Bible reading, meditating on Scripture, worshipping, and sitting still before Him, the Lord begins to change and shape our desires to match His. It's only then that we can claim promises like the one below.

FAITHFULLY HIS

> *"Delight yourself also in the* LORD,
> *And He shall give you the desires of your heart."*
> Psalm 37:4 NKJV

Recently, I was believing God to make provision for me to go to Rwanda to visit the little girl that I have been sponsoring for six years through Compassion International. I needed $3,790 in order to take the 10-day trip to Kigali, and I did not have that type of money just sitting around in my bank account. However, I strongly felt that this was something I was supposed to do, and it was an opportunity for my faith to be tested to see if I would trust God to provide. The Scripture that the Lord led me to is Psalm 34:10 (NKJV):

> *"The young lions lack and suffer hunger, but those who seek the* LORD *shall not lack any good thing."*

By the grace of God, I was able to pay the $380 trip deposit on April 16th, which was a big step of faith. The deadline to pay the remaining balance of $3,410 was May 3rd, and I had no idea where any of it would come from. I felt crazy and out of my comfort zone. I remember telling the Lord that if He did not come through, I would be out $380. In His loving kindness, He kept leading me to Scriptures to stand on. When I sought Him for direction on what steps to take, I kept being led to Psalm 46:10, *"Be still and know that I am God."* Anybody who knows me knows that I do not like to be still, yet God was challenging me to do that very thing.

WHAT HAS GOD PROMISED?

I prayed, fasted, and let certain people around me know what I was believing God for and solicited their prayers. The day before the deadline, one of my dearest friends reached out and donated $150, which was all the confirmation I needed to know that God was going to work this out. This particular friend is a prayer warrior and woman of faith who doesn't make a move unless she is led by the Lord to do so. I began to sing and praise God in advance for what He was about to do. Well, the next day came and went, and I was still $3,260 short. As I looked to God for answers, He continued to place Psalm 34:10 on my heart.

A friend suggested that I reach out and ask for an extension, which I was honestly embarrassed by at first and thought for sure my request would be declined. Right before I wrote the email, I was led to read a devotional that had been sent to my inbox the night before. I almost shouted for joy when I saw that the highlighted Scripture was the same one that the Lord had been leading me to all week: Psalm 34:10! If I'm honest, at first, I was just going to be vague and ask for a few days, but I felt the Lord impress upon my heart that I needed to be specific and ask for a week. I sent an email to the group leader for the trip and asked God for His perfect will to be done in requesting an extension until the 11th. To my surprise, they honored my request, but they also asked if I could send a minimum of $380 over the weekend so that they could purchase my airfare, which required $1,000.

I was in shock and immediately ran to tell my co-worker the great news! I had just received donations totaling $500 from people who wanted to help. Even though I was still short about $2,760, I knew that this was God testing my faith but also showing me that He surely would provide the rest. I continued to stand on His Word and truly saw the salvation of the Lord when a lady whom I had never met donated $2,200 to me through PayPal. After that, it was only a matter of time before the Lord sent people to donate the last few hundred dollars. In fact, I ended up having more money than I needed and was able to buy a plane ticket back to Dallas for my return trip.

That experience showed me exactly what God promises in His Word: He is faithful. We never have to fear that He won't come through on what He says. He is not a man, so He cannot lie. Point blank period. End of story.

God has consistently shown me in other seasons of my life that He is faithful to provide for my needs. When the Lord led me to move to Texas in January of 2016, it was a total faith move, as I had no job or true idea of why I was moving. All I knew was that God had confirmed it and given me peace that surpassed all understanding. I didn't know it at the time, but the journey He would take me on would cause me to realize how truly powerful His promises are for those who believe. There were many times when I had to trust Him when I couldn't see how things were going to work out for me. I had to choose to believe Him and His Word over my feelings and emotions. I learned that my circumstances could no longer be a sign of God's love for me. There were days when I literally had $0.00 in the bank, and all I had were the promises of God to stand on. I had to continually tell myself that God's grace was sufficient enough to carry me through even the toughest circumstances. My situation was not based upon anything I did or didn't do, but God was trying to teach me to be satisfied with Him alone. When I look back at that season I can testify that I never went without and my dependency on and faith in Him increased tremendously. God's provision often showed up in the most unconventional ways and moments, which I will discuss more in Chapter 16, but He always came through. The Lord taught me in those moments that wherever He calls us He will provide for us.

Rest in His promises, and He will supply exactly what you need in His timing and in His perfect way!

Time to Reflect

1. What promises do you need to stand and meditate on this week?
2. What is God calling you to believe Him for in this season? Ask the Lord to lead you to 2 passages of Scriptures that line up with that and use them during your time of prayer.

"But those who wait on the Lord
Shall renew their strength;
They shall mount up with wings like eagles,
They shall run and not be weary,
They shall walk and not faint."
Isaiah 40:31 NKJV

11

TRUSTING GOD WHEN HE SAYS "NO"

> *"'My thoughts are nothing like your thoughts,' says the Lord. 'And my ways are far beyond anything you could imagine. For just as the heavens are higher than the earth, so my ways are higher than your ways and my thoughts higher than your thoughts.'"*
> Isaiah 55:8-9 NLT

As humans, we cannot see what lies ahead in the future. We can assume or try to predict what might happen, but only God knows exactly what the future holds for each and every one of us. His ways are far above our comprehension, and His plan is perfect, even though, at times, it may seem like the opposite is true. The world is constantly telling us, "it's your life, do what makes you happy" and "follow your heart," but those paths ultimately lead to self-destruction.

As Christians, we don't have a life to take control of because we gave our lives to Christ when we accepted Him as Lord and

Savior. And even though our hearts have been cleansed by the blood of Jesus, they still have the potential to deceive us and lead us astray. We naturally want to operate by sight instead of faith and to have complete control of our lives. We don't want to wait for anything and often think that we know what's best. It takes faith, trust, and humility to believe that God knows best and that we don't know everything, but it's not always easy to hear that.

We currently live in what I like to call a "microwave society." Advances in technology have allowed for us to have access to things at a click of a button. Everything is instant these days from how we shop to how we cook our food and how we communicate with each other. We are so used to having access to anything and everything we want as quickly as we want it that we have a hard time exercising patience or accepting rejection. So, it's no wonder that we tend to project that into our relationship with the Lord. I have heard some people say that God's answer is always "yes" and "amen." Well, I do not know if they are talking about the God that I serve because there have been times when He was quick to say "no" to me when my desires were outside of His plan. I could tell story after story about times when I really wanted to do something, move on from something, quit, or go somewhere, and God told me "no." They weren't necessarily "bad things" either, but He still said "no."

There are also countless stories in the Bible where God told people "no," and if He is the same yesterday, today, and forever, then He still says "no." It is proof of His unfailing love for us because He wants and knows what is best for us.

God tells us "no" for a bunch of different reasons, but I'll just highlight a few:

1. *To protect us from harm.*
2. *To showcase His glory through the troubles that we are currently facing.*
3. *To keep us available and in position for something greater.*
4. *To draw us into a deeper relationship with Him.*
5. *To discipline us.*
6. *To prepare us for the future.*

One example of this is found in the life of Paul in 2 Corinthians 12:7-10 (NLT):

"So to keep me from becoming proud, I was given a thorn in my flesh, a messenger from Satan to torment me and keep me from becoming proud. Three different times I begged the Lord to take it away. Each time he said, 'My grace is all you need. My power works best in weakness.' So now I am glad to boast about my weaknesses, so that the power of Christ can work through me. That's why I take pleasure in my weaknesses, and in the insults, hardships, persecutions, and troubles that I suffer for Christ. For when I am weak, then I am strong."

In the above passage, Paul went to God three different times asking Him to take away his affliction, but God said "no." He had a purpose and a reason behind it, even though it probably didn't make sense to Paul. I'm sure Paul would have preferred a problem-free life, but God wanted to use the thorn to showcase His own glory. He knew that the pain would keep Paul humble and keep him from becoming self-sufficient. As a result, Paul had no choice but to grow spiritually and mature in the Lord. I'm also sure his prayer life also deepened as he leaned on the Lord to see him through.

Although sometimes it is hard for us to comprehend, God truly does know what is best. He has plans for our lives and knows which doors need to be closed in order for us to stay focused and on the straight and narrow path. I know that, sometimes, when we really want something, or even someone, and God says "no," we can get upset and frustrated. What we must realize is that we are looking at whatever it is from an earthly perspective. Meanwhile, God is looking at it from an eternal perspective and can see the end from the beginning. We have to ask God to renew our minds so that we may see things from His perspective. He is not saying "no" to punish you but to protect you. Either what you are asking for will bring you harm, or you just aren't ready to handle that which you are requesting.

Instead of complaining, we need to be celebrating that God loves us enough to keep us from things that could potentially knock us off course. He cares so much for our well-being that He doesn't want us to experience unnecessary hurt, failure, or pain.

"...I have cared for you since you were born. Yes, I carried you before you were born. I will be your God throughout your lifetime-until your hair is white with age. I made you, and I will care for you. I will carry you along and save you."
Isaiah 46:3-4 NKJV

"Or what man is there among you who, when his son asks for a loaf, will give him a stone? Or if he asks for a fish, he will not give him a snake, will he? If you then, being evil, know how to give good gifts to your children, how much more will your Father who is in heaven give what is good to those who ask Him!"
Matthew 7:9-11 NASB

A few years ago, there was this guy at the church I was attending whom everyone thought I should be talking to. I prayed about it and immediately sensed the Lord saying "no." Before I could even get the words out, I had an uneasy feeling in the pit of my stomach. God's answer hurt my feelings. I thought, "Lord, I have been single for so long, and then when I do actually meet someone attractive and a Christian, you say 'no.' That doesn't make sense." I truly sensed the Holy Spirit whispering, "I have someone better in mind." I can be a bit stubborn, so I continued to ask the Lord over and over again about this particular guy until He pretty much removed the guy from my life altogether. One day, we were friends, and the next day, I found out that he was going back to his old church in a different part of town. It's not that he was a "bad" guy or not a devout Christian, but only God knows the path that He has ordained for me. Who knows what the outcome may have been if I had chosen to ignore God's instructions or had I never prayed about it at all. Who knows if I would have been able to fulfill all the plans that God has for me. It didn't matter how many people thought it was a good idea; God said "no" because He has someone and something else better for me in mind. In His omniscience, the Lord can see the end from the beginning and loved me enough to let me know that was not the path He desired me to walk down.

There have been so many times when I applied for jobs, went through the interview process, went to accept the offer, but never received a response back. Then, there have been times when God shut down the whole process before I even went to the interviews. Do you know how frustrating it is to need a job and finally find a job, only to have to decline it? I would sit there confused and upset, but a few days, weeks, or months later, a better offer and opportunity would present itself, and I was thankful that I was free to take the job.

Friend, let me tell you something: you do not know what is on the other side of God's "no." You may be settling for something or someone, but God wants to take you higher and actually give you more. Or maybe He wants to use you in a different way than you anticipated. He is sovereign over every detail of our lives, and we cannot afford to make decisions solely based on what we see, feel, and hear in the natural realm. As His children, we do have free will, but the Lord has also given us the Holy Spirit to help teach and guide us through life. Every decision that we are led to make will not always make sense to our finite minds. It is important that we continually ask the Lord to help us trust Him and stop trying to figure things out on our own. Otherwise, we may drive ourselves crazy trying to play God and understand His infinite knowledge and wisdom with our small, finite minds.

Here are a few Scriptures that help portray just how much God is thinking about us and wants to direct our steps.

"Trust in the Lord with all your heart; do not depend on your own understanding. Seek his will in all you do, and he will show you which path to take."
Proverbs 3:5-6 NLT

"How precious are your thoughts about me, O God. They cannot be numbered! I can't even count them; they outnumber the grains of sand. And when I wake up, you are still with me!"
Psalm 139:17-18 NLT

TRUSTING GOD WHEN HE SAYS "NO"

"For the LORD watches over the path of the godly."
Psalm 1:6 NLT

The Lord literally sits in heaven and watches over us. He can see that car that almost hit us, but His angels blocked it. He can see that if we take that job, we will end up getting entangled in a legal battle. He can see that if we move to that state, we will end up going astray in our Christian walk. He can see that if we become friends with that person, they will draw us away from Christ. He can see that if we go to that party, there will be a shooting. He can see that if we enter that business deal, we will lose all of our assets. We have to remember that when we go to God in prayer to ask Him questions, we cannot have our own hidden agenda. James 1:5-8 (NLT) says it best:

"But if any of you lacks wisdom, let him ask of God, who gives to all generously and without reproach, and it will be given to him. But he must ask in faith without any doubting, for the one who doubts is like the surf of the sea, driven and tossed by the wind. For that man ought not to expect that he will receive anything from the Lord, being a double-minded man, unstable in all his ways."

Our Heavenly Father is willing and able to give us wisdom and direction for any situation or problem we may face, but we must be open to receiving His direction—whatever it may be. When we begin to truly trust God, we are able to see that He always has our best interest at heart. The next time you seek the Lord and He says "no," don't get upset; instead, rejoice and give Him praise. He just saved you from something and is redirecting you to something or someone else that is better suited for you.

If you feel like you are seeking the Lord and not seeing, hearing, or receiving a response at all, remember that a delay is not a denial. Your Heavenly Father wants to give you an answer, but we must also make sure we ask with the right motives. There are different reasons for the delays we experience in getting our prayers answered. We must ask God to search our hearts and reveal to us any unconfessed sin or unforgiveness in our hearts. Sometimes God will delay His answer to develop patience and persistence within us that will build our faith. Other times, it is an invitation to go deeper with God and create a stronger bond of intimacy between us and Him. Also, we must be open to how He may respond, because the Lord communicates in many different ways. Primarily through His Word, but also through the Holy Spirit, dreams, visions, wisdom from others, sermons, nature, and the list goes on. One thing to note is that whenever and however God chooses to communicate with us, He will never contradict His Word. The Lord wants to give us His best, but we must wait on Him in order to receive it. Instead of going to Him with our own agendas, we must get into the practice of asking that His will be done above all else.

> *"Your kingdom come.*
> *Your will be done*
> *On earth as it is in heaven"*
> *Matthew 6:10 NKJV*

God is truly a good Father. The very nature of God is goodness and perfection. He is good because He is God, and He is God because He is good. The Lord is always looking out for us and delights in answering our prayers. If we could just get ourselves out of the way and look at life from His perspective, then we would see that His answers to our prayers are perfect, whether that answer is "yes," "no," or "not yet."

If you take nothing else from this chapter, I want you to remember the following:

God is GOOD!
God is PERFECT!
God is WITH YOU!
God is FOR YOU!
God will NEVER LEAD YOU ASTRAY!

So instead of putting your trust in creation (man, things, and this world), put your trust in the Creator. Our journey with Christ is not always going to make sense. We aren't always going to understand why God lets certain things happen, but if we trust Him, we will see His perfect plan unfold. The Lord loves you and me enough to tell us, "no," and I'm grateful for that.

Time to Reflect

1. What are some of the instances in which the Lord has spared you from making a decision that would have ended badly?
2. Take time to thank God for all of the doors that He has closed in your life and for His protective hand guiding you.

> *"Thus says the Lord, your Redeemer,*
> *The Holy One of Israel:*
> *'I am the Lord your God,*
> *Who teaches you to profit,*
> *Who leads you by the way you should go.'"*
> *Isaiah 48:17 NKJV*

12

FEAR NOT

"For God has not given us a spirit of fear, but of power and of love and of a sound mind."
2 Timothy 1:7 NKJV

Fear is a liar, but it feels very real. If it is not handled properly, fear can really ruin our walks with the Lord. As we see above, in 2 Timothy 1:7, the Bible tells us that God is not the author of fear.

Now, there is a difference between the holy, reverent fear of God (1 Samuel 12:24, 1 Peter 1:17) that we should have as believers and the terrifying, anxious, worrisome type of fear. The second type of fear I mentioned is evil and of the Devil. We are to cast it down (2 Corinthians 5:10) and not entertain it. If we allow the Enemy to gain a foothold into our minds and lives, he will take over and potentially paralyze us from moving forward in our Christian walk. He loves to plant seeds of doubt, fear, and negativity in our minds to distract and discourage us as well as magnify small issues in our lives to make them seem impossible to overcome or to divide us from others.

Sometimes, the issues the Devil brings to our attention aren't actually even issues at all but just made up in our head. We will spend precious time pondering the "what-if's" of life and all of the potential negative outcomes of a situation. If we aren't careful, we will find ourselves losing trust and hope in God. This is especially true as it pertains to living by faith. Fear creates doubt in our minds, which dampens our faith and often causes us to forget how sovereign God is. In times of uncertainty or adversity, the Enemy wants us to forget that God has come through for us before and attempts to convince us that God has forgotten about us. As I mentioned before, we serve a God whose thoughts about us outnumber the grains of sand (Psalm 139:18) and who had every day of our lives recorded in His Book before we were even born (Psalm 139:16). There is not one thing about us or our lives that catches Him by surprise, which should give us the confidence and assurance that we need to walk in faith instead of fear. How many of you know that, despite that truth, we are still prone to find ourselves in situations that cause fear and doubt in our hearts?

In my journey of faith, the Lord has often called me to take leaps of faith into the unknown, whether it meant quitting a job or moving to a new state. As I mentioned earlier, in 2016, the Lord called me to leave my place of comfort and familiarity in Atlanta, Georgia and move to Dallas, Texas. Although, initially, I had no idea what I would do or where I would live when I got there, I had a supernatural peace about the transition. A few weeks before I was supposed to move to Dallas, though, I started having panic attacks in the middle of the night, which went on for five nights in a row. Like clockwork every night, about 1am or 2am, I would wake up and begin to feel as if the walls were caving in on me. As my heartbeat began to intensify, I suddenly would be filled with terror as negative images flooded my mind. I sat there paralyzed by the following thoughts and questions:

> *"What am I doing?"*
> *"What if I get there and nothing happens?"*
> *"What if I missed God?"*
> *"You don't have to move; God is lying to you."*
> *"God really didn't say all of that."*
> *"You are going to move, and nothing is going to work out."*

Honestly, for the first few days, I didn't even notice the pattern and would wake up, panic, and then drift off back to sleep within a few minutes. However, by the fifth night, I realized what was happening to me. That night, I decided to attend a worship night with a friend of mine. As I postured my heart before the Lord, He began to show me all the seeds of doubt and fear that I had allowed the Enemy to plant in my heart that week. It was hindering my walk with the Lord and killing my faith drastically. By not fighting back, I was giving the Enemy an opportunity to "devour" me in my weakened state (1 Peter 5:8). He reminded me that this battle we face as Christians is purely spiritual, just as it tells us in Ephesians 6:12 (NKJV):

> *"For we do not wrestle against flesh and blood, but against principalities, against powers, against the rulers of the darkness of this age, against spiritual hosts of wickedness in the heavenly places."*

Once the Lord revealed to me where the attacks were coming from, I was better able to fight back. I needed to put on the full armor of God and stand firm instead of just allowing the fiery darts of the Enemy overtake me (Ephesians 6:11-17). That night, when the attack came, I heard the Enemy whisper the lie, "I am going to devour you." By this time, I was done with his foolishness, and instead of panicking, I began to say over and over again, "Perfect love casts out all fear!"

"There is no fear in love; but perfect love casts out fear, because fear involves torment. But he who fears has not been made perfect in love."
1 John 4:18 NKJV

I also found myself reciting Psalm 23:4 (NKJV):

"Yea, though I walk through the valley of the shadow of death, I will fear no evil; For You are with me; Your rod and Your staff, they comfort me."

Immediately, I felt at peace and went back to sleep. The next day, when I was at a Bible study for the dance ministry at my church, I told the women what I had been experiencing, and they prayed for me. I haven't had those types of nighttime attacks since then, and that experience taught me just how full of lies the Enemy is. Everything about him is a lie, including the shadows he tries to create in our lives to cause us to live in fear. He knows that if he can get a few Christians to step out of the will of God by blanketing them in fear, then fewer people will come to the knowledge and truth of who God is. He literally studies us, knows our weaknesses, and plots on when to strike.

However, we must remember that the truth is not in him, and he cannot harm our souls or take away our salvation.

"You are of your father the devil, and the desires of your father you want to do. He was a murderer from the beginning, and does not stand in the truth, because there is no truth in him. When he speaks a lie, he speaks from his own resources, for he is a liar and the father of it."
John 8:44 NKJV

Shortly after that incident, the Lord reminded me that the Enemy tried the same type of spiritual warfare tactics before I moved to Atlanta from New York City in 2013. That season of intense warfare lasted for over 10 months because I was unaware of what was happening and why. I didn't fully understand the spiritual power that God has given His children to overcome the schemes and plots of the Enemy. Fast forward to the present day, and I'm wiser, I'm stronger, I'm better, I'm more equipped, and I am not playing games with the Enemy! I know where my help comes from, and Jesus is greater than all! Does that mean the attacks have subsided in my life? Absolutely not! If anything, they are often more intense in this current season, but I am encouraged to know that God is with me through it all and that when I feel weak and defeated, He is strong (2 Corinthians 12:9).

The Enemy only attacks those by whom he feels threatened. Once we said "yes" to God, you and I became perfect targets for him. There are going to be times in this Christian journey when we fall prey to his fear tactics, but we can't stay down. We have to remember where the attacks come from, seek the Lord, and get back up. There are going to be times when we will be tempted to give up or go astray, but quitting is not an option. You are not helpless or hopeless; you are victorious through Christ Jesus! Other people are counting on your ability to endure through the tests and trials that come your way. You have a calling on your life that not even the attacks of the Enemy can thwart. It is our faith in God's perfect and unconditional love for us, demonstrated through Christ's sacrifice, that helps us to rise above fear. We can rest assured that God has already won the victory, and all He is asking for us to do is stand on His truth. All He is asking for you to do is be still and wait patiently for Him to act (Psalm 37:7). Even if your struggle isn't fear, just know that whatever it is, you are an overcomer through the blood of Jesus Christ. The battle was won 2,000 years ago at Calvary, but it's up to you walk in that victory today! It's up to you to put on the whole armor of God and fight back when the attacks come. Fight for your peace of mind! Fight for your joy! Fight for your endurance!

 I didn't know exactly what God had in store for me in Texas at that time, but I refused to let the Enemy distract me and knock me off course. He continuously attacked my mind with fear as a few well-meaning friends and family expressed their concerns and doubts about my transition to Texas. But as I kept on running the race and continuously asking God for strength to endure until the end, the Lord was faithful to bring comfort, joy, confirmation, and peace through many other family and friends. Now that I am on the other side of everything, I see exactly why the Enemy wanted to keep me from moving to Dallas. The impact and influence that I am able to have on others in my current position is nothing but the work of God. Even though saying "yes" to God in that transition was hard and uncomfortable, I'm glad that His presence and Word equipped me to walk by faith and not by sight, to live by faith and not by fear. Looking back, God did exactly what He said He would do, and I wasted so much valuable time worrying about what He had in store. Through my transition to Texas, God taught me that He's going to move and open doors in His perfect timing and not a moment sooner. We do not have to fear the seasons of change and transition because our God is the Alpha and the Omega, the Beginning and the End.

I can admit that not knowing exactly what will happen can be nerve-wracking at times, but when we put our faith in our Heavenly Father, we don't have to fret about the unknown. He has a perfect plan for each and every one of us. When we walk by faith, God gets maximum glory through our lives, and people are drawn to Him. It causes others to see that the seemingly impossible becomes possible with God. Faith and fear don't mix any more than praying and worrying do. We have to choose one or the other. Today, will you choose faith? Will you choose to be strong and courageous (Joshua 1:9)? Will you choose to endure until the end (Matthew 24:13), knowing that God has a purpose and plan for all that He allows?

Whatever you are holding onto or allowing into your life that is causing you to live in a state of fear, I encourage you to lay it all down at the feet of Jesus because He truly does care for you (1 Peter 5:7). Yield those thoughts and worries to the Lord and allow His perfect peace to guard your heart and mind in Christ Jesus (Philippians 4:7).

Time to Reflect

1. What are some areas of fear in your life?
2. How will you move forward in submitting your fears to the Lord and walking in victory over them?
3. Find three Scriptures that pertain to your situation and recite them out loud every time you are tempted to walk in fear instead of faith.

> *"It is the LORD who goes before you. He will be with you; he will not leave you nor forsake you. Do not fear or be dismayed."*
> *Deuteronomy 31:8 ESV*

Part 6

ENDURING THE VALLEY

13

TRUSTING GOD IN SEASONS OF HARDSHIP

"For our light affliction, which is but for a moment, is working for us a far more exceeding and eternal weight of glory, while we do not look at the things which are seen, but at the things which are not seen. For the things which are seen are temporary, but the things which are not seen are eternal."
2 Corinthians 4:17-18 NKJV

Evicted.

In September of 2016, I had to move out of my apartment because I was evicted. Yes, the apartment that I just moved into at the end of May. Yes, the apartment that I know the Lord led me to. Yes, the apartment that I had prayed and fasted over throughout the entire leasing process. I had even walked around the whole complex and prayed over it before I even moved in. Yes, the apartment that contained every single thing on the list that I had brought before the Lord and more.

Yes, the apartment that was only a 15-minute drive from my current job like I had asked of the Lord. Yes, the apartment that I was supposed to be hosting prayer nights, worship nights, and Bible studies in. Yes, the apartment that God miraculously provided the necessary funds to pay my rent for the previous two months.

Not only that, but I strongly felt the Lord tugging on my heart to leave my job as well. Saying that I was distraught was an understatement. Not only was I being forced to move; I could no longer count on my job for income. I was so confused and didn't understand why it seemed like God was taking away everything that I had prayed for. It would have been different if I had just done my own thing, but I had actively sought Him throughout the whole process. In my eyes, it looked like everything in life was literally falling apart, and I found myself questioning God's goodness. How could this be God's will for my life? To be jobless and homeless at the same time? My faith fell to an all-time low as disappointment swelled in my heart. This was not how I saw it all ending. Every other month, God had come through in the midnight hour, but this time, it seemed like the heavens were closed, and His provision was nowhere in sight. I had given up everything to move to Texas only months earlier and couldn't see how this could be a part of His plan. Surely, He had turned His back on me. I had faced trials and tribulations before but never to this extent.

Prior to receiving the final eviction notice, I had spent hours upon hours in prayer, and it honestly seemed like He was going to come through. My hopes and faith were high, and I had this surreal peace about the situation. I remember walking around that morning and telling the Lord that I had faith like Abraham and believed that if He took my apartment away from me, then He could revive the situation and give it back. Well, God took me seriously because I wasn't able to come up with all of the money by the deadline. In fact, later that day, I rushed into the leasing office with a money order, to cover the full amount due, only to hear one of the leasing consultants tell me that the property manager had just left to file the final eviction paperwork.

As I sat in the office on the verge of tears, my hopes and faith were shattered, but there was also a quiet peace in my soul. I knew God was capable, and I couldn't understand why He didn't just do it. Looking back, I can honestly say that God did provide for me even though it wasn't financially (the way I expected). He provided me with friends who stayed late into the night to help me pack up my apartment and parents who covered the costs of a U-Haul and storage unit. He gave me friends who were conveniently free to help me move my stuff in the middle of the day and a place to lay my head that night. Of course, none of this was running through my mind at the time; I was too much of a mess to fully recognize God's sovereign and loving hand at work.

I don't think I've felt more abandoned, forsaken, or embarrassed in my life than at that moment. I felt like I had trusted God, done everything He told me to, and still came up short. It's amazing how God's mercy and grace was demonstrated through it all—how He never stopped loving me even when I turned my back on Him. In my ignorance, I thought I had somehow thwarted God's plan for my life, but it still remained intact. I thought that maybe I had missed a step somewhere and that this was my punishment for not being obedient. I would later learn that God wanted to birth something new in my life and was just using this experience to do so.

I wish I could say that I was thankful, but at the time, my heart had become so hardened towards God. For the next few days, I pretty much avoided sitting still and spending any time with Him. Instead, I cried, cried, and cried some more (if you know me, you know I rarely cry, so that's a big deal). I tried to keep myself busy so that I wouldn't have to deal with the reality of what had just happened, which seemed like the end of the world. I couldn't see how I could ever recover from this type of loss. Obviously, I had "missed God" and felt so purposeless that I seriously considered moving to another city or state to start over again.

If it hadn't been for a faithful few who called to pray with me and encourage me, I would not have made it through those first couple of days. I was beating myself up with a "shoulda, coulda, woulda" attitude, and the Enemy was having a complete field day with me. I felt so weak and was just plain tired. I lost the assurance that I could even receive instructions and guidance from the Holy Spirit. Even though my feelings and emotions were all over the place, I had a sense in my spirit that God was still there. It's like I knew better in my spirit, but my flesh was doing the most.

Despite all of the confusion, I can honestly say that God never stopped pursuing me. I'm thankful for His constant love, grace, and mercy towards me. Looking back, I see that He was constantly encouraging me not to quit by sending friends, sermons, songs, and Scriptures across my path. When I finally took time to sit before God and just be still, I thought He was going to rebuke me for purposely avoiding Him, but instead, He welcomed me with loving arms. As I confessed the hardness of my heart and my feelings and asked Him to forgive me, He drew me near to Him. The Lord showed me that He had me in that season for a reason and graced me with the ability to trust that He was truly sovereign. When things do not go as I planned, I learned that my Heavenly Father is still in control and working behind the scenes for me. The hardships I faced in that season were an invitation to rest in the Lord and go deeper in my walk with Him. My life didn't make much sense, but I chose to rest on the promises of God to sustain and pull me through.

Even though I had no income coming in, God still always made a way. I had people reach out to me right after I'd spent hours in prayer and fasting saying that the Lord laid it on their hearts to sow into me. Throughout that ordeal, I was blessed to stay in the homes of six different sisters in Christ, all for free.

Now, let me say this, it wasn't until recently that I was able to see many of these blessings. At first, I felt super unstable moving from place to place, not really knowing who was going to say "yes" next. I also had a hard time receiving from others because I'm used to being the one who gives. I had to pray and ask God to give me His perspective on all of these things. But once I surrendered this entire situation over to God, I began to see the pattern of His provision, protection, and direction. No, it definitely was not what I thought my journey in Texas would be like, but even in that, I learned to be content and grateful.

There I was, 27, single, without a job or stable housing, and bills piling up by the minute, which doesn't exactly sound appealing. According to the American Dream and society's standards, I was failing miserably, but in God's eyes, I know that He couldn't be happier that I had chosen Him and His path. Success in God's Kingdom is obedience to Him no matter how unconventional that path may seem. Honestly, I'm glad that the Lord didn't show me this side of the journey beforehand because, otherwise, I would probably still be living in Atlanta right now all outside of His will. He knows me so well, and He showed me the good first so that it would be an encouragement to help me endure the ashes that have to come before the beauty.

One of the biggest lessons I learned throughout this was to PERSEVERE! The Lord sent so many women my way to love on, encourage, and pray with, even in the midst of my own struggles. It taught me to think of others more than I think of myself and to die to my flesh. It taught me that true ministry is caring for others and trusting that God will take care of you. It taught me that when trouble comes, it's not the time to draw inward and isolate yourself but to keep your eyes on Christ and surround yourself with other believers who are strong in their faith.

In that season, I was able to read Christian books and study the Bible for prolonged amounts of time, which I wouldn't have been able to do if I was working. I was better able to construct my days around Christ instead of just squeezing Him in for a brief moment here and there. I knew that it was just a season of rest, and soon, the Lord would send me back out into His harvest to do His work, so I tried to take advantage of every single moment.

The Lord taught me to speak life and not death over my situation, to pray and not complain when things got tough. God showed me the benefits of what some Christians call P.U.S.H. (Praying Until Something Happens). Our world is so fast-paced that we sometimes carry that over into our prayer lives and give up when we don't see instant results. As I sat still before the Lord in that season, He taught me the true meaning of prayer.

I discovered that there is nothing that brings more joy than to labor in prayer for the needs of others, as well as yourself, and see God actually answer those prayers. To pray in faith, with no doubting, and witness how God chooses to answer those prayers is an amazing thing. To pray and then, by faith, praise God in advance for answering your prayer, even though you cannot see the results in the natural yet, is pleasing to God. I could go on and on about all the lessons that I learned, but just know that He often places us in seasons of transition so that He can prepare our hearts and minds for where we will go next. He's not punishing you by taking you through the valley but pruning you for greater service for Him. God truly has a plan for our lives, and we can be confident that His eyes are always upon us in both the good and bad times.

> *"The eyes of the LORD are in every place, Keeping watch on the evil and the good."*
> Proverbs 15:3 NKJV

As you walk by faith, there are some seasons when you literally have to trust Him for your daily bread. There are other seasons when you will have an abundance to share with others. You are not loved more by God if you are in a season of abundance, and you are not loved less by Him if you are in a season of lack or just enough. Each season serves a purpose in your growth and development as a Christian. The goal is to make us more like Christ by any means necessary. God knows what we need to experience and when we need to experience it so that we will grow into the fullness of Christ. The process of sanctification isn't pretty, but the results bring glory to God and prepare us for eternity.

Your journey is uniquely yours, so don't compare yourself to anyone else. Just look to God and seek His face. I don't know if you are currently in the wilderness or reaping the harvest of the Promise Land, but just know that God loves you. Your story is not just for you but to help someone else come into the knowledge of our Lord and Savior, Jesus Christ. A few of the Scriptures that gave me encouragement and strength in that season of transition are:

> *"Naked I came from my mother's womb, And naked I shall return there. The LORD gave, and the LORD has taken away; Blessed be the name of the LORD."*
> *Job 1:21 NKJV*

> *"You will keep him in perfect peace, Whose mind is stayed on You, Because he trusts in You. Trust in the LORD forever, For in YAH, the LORD is everlasting strength."*
> *Isaiah 26:3-4 NKJV*

> *"But may the God of all grace, who called us to His eternal glory by Christ Jesus, after you have suffered a while, perfect, establish, strengthen, and settle you."*
> *1 Peter 5:10 NKJV*

TRUSTING GOD IN SEASONS OF HARDSHIP

"Many are the afflictions of the righteous, But the LORD delivers him out of them all."
Psalm 34:19 NKJV

"'...Not by might nor by power, but by My Spirit,' Says the Lord of hosts."
Zechariah 4:6 NKJV

"And He said to me, 'My grace is sufficient for you, for My strength is made perfect in weakness.' Therefore most gladly I will rather boast in my infirmities, that the power of Christ may rest upon me. Therefore I take pleasure in infirmities, in reproaches, in needs, in persecutions, in distresses, for Christ's sake. For when I am weak, then I am strong."
2 Corinthians 12:9-10 NKJV

"And let us not grow weary while doing good, for in due season we shall reap if we do not lose heart."
Galatians 6:9 NKJV

Psalm 34 and Psalm 91

May the words of our Lord serve as a source of comfort, peace, faith, hope, and strength as you navigate through the hard seasons of life and remind you just how much you are loved and cared for.

Time to Reflect

1. What are some instances in your life in which you chose to trust God in spite of what your current circumstances looked like?
2. How did those situations above turn out for you? Did God deliver you? Did God provide for you? Did God heal you? Did God change your perspective on your circumstances? Take some time to thank Him for His sovereign hand at work in your life.

3. What are some Scriptures that you can stand on to help carry you through a future hardship that may arise?
4. Moving forward, how will you combat your feelings and emotions with truth in the midst of a problem?

> *"Cast your burden on the Lord, And He shall sustain you; He shall never permit the righteous to be moved."*
> *Psalm 55:22 NKJV*

14

REMAINING FAITHFUL THROUGH SUFFERING

*"Even though Jesus was God's Son, he learned obedience
from the things he suffered."*
Hebrews 5:8 NLT

Whether you are a follower of Jesus or not, life is hard. We live in broken world that is tainted by sin and full of tragedies, sorrows, and iniquities. Some are caused by our sin, some are caused by the sin of others, and some are allowed by God's design for a greater purpose. Going through that season of hardship taught me a truth that I had never fully grasped until then.

God's demonstration of love can also be found in times of suffering or hardship.

The Lord loves us enough to welcome us into His family as we are, but He will not let us remain the same. We were created in His image, and He desires to see His glory displayed through us. The problem is that we have a sinful nature that is constantly at odds with the Spirit of God who dwells within us (Galatians 5:17). Our Heavenly Father will allow a hardship to come our way so that we can be refined and purified. It is in that hard place that He is able to prune, shape, and mold us in ways that only He can. Just like diamonds are created under pressure, we, too, are able to bloom into our greatest potential as God cuts back the lies, deceit, and sin that are revealed to be within us when we are in seasons of hardship or great testing. In these moments, what we say we believe is put to the test, and we have no other option but to look up to the Lord. It is in that place of dependency on Him that we mature and grow into the likeness of Christ. There are some seasons of our lives where it may seem like we are being tested daily with no relief in sight (I'm sure I am not the only one who can testify to that). Then, there are some seasons when everything seems to be perfectly okay, which is when we are often tempted to become more self-sufficient and less dependent on God.

As I mentioned earlier, we cannot allow our temporal circumstances to dictate our beliefs about God's power, goodness, or love. We must be rooted and grounded in Him enough to be able to say, "God is good all the time, and all the time God is good." From my experience, it's often in times of intense suffering that we begin to realize, or are reminded, that our greatest need is to have more of Jesus. It doesn't matter if you have been walking with God for six months or 60 years; we are all "prone to wander,"[xvii] as the old hymn says. When things are going well, it is so easy to make idols out of the gifts the Lord has given us, but when issues and problems arise, we are quickly reminded that God is the all-sufficient One and is essential to our livelihood. We are reminded that God is the most perfect gift that we could ever receive. As we navigate through the ups and downs of life, we also have an opportunity to see and examine if our love for God is genuine or not. Are we just bandwagon fans, or are we committed followers? It's easy to love God when everything is going our way, but when we are at rock bottom, there is a human inclination to wonder if God truly cares. That is why it's so important that we follow and stand on truth—even if our feelings or emotions aren't initially onboard (if we stand firm, they will eventually catch up).

Think about this: Jesus suffered until the point of death and displayed the greatest act of love known to humankind. It was God's will for Him to suffer. Let me repeat that: it was God's will for His only Son to suffer. There was an outcome that God needed, and it could only have come through the crucifixion of Jesus. He showed us that through our suffering and sacrifices, there is an opportunity to learn a deeper level of obedience to God and for His glory to be put on display. We can remain faithful to God in intense seasons of suffering because Jesus Himself did first.

There are many times in which God uses the tests and trials of life to get our attention and point us back to Him. Unfortunately, there are many believers out there who have been told that if they walk with God, then they will never face hard times, which couldn't be further from the truth found in Scripture. Even I went through a period of time in which I used to carry myself as if I deserved to be exempt from bad experiences because I was a daughter of the King and had my daily quiet time. Then one day I read Philippians 2:5-11 (ESV):

"Have this mind among yourselves, which is yours in Christ Jesus, who, though he was in the form of God, did not count equality with God a thing to be grasped, but emptied himself, by taking the form of a servant, being

born in the likeness of men. And being found in human form, he humbled himself by becoming obedient to the point of death, even death on a cross. Therefore, God has highly exalted him and bestowed on him the name that is above every name, so that at the name of Jesus every knee should bow, in heaven and on earth and under the earth, and every tongue confess that Jesus Christ is Lord, to the glory of God the Father."

Whoa. Talk about a humbling moment for repentance. If Jesus, the Son of God, disregarded His equality with God in order to fulfill the mission that was laid before Him, which included dying on the cross, then how could I (a mere human) expect to be exempt from bad experiences? Again, this is why good theology is so important to our daily walks with the Lord. You and I are not on the same level as Jesus, and if He was willing to walk in obedience, even though that meant enduring through suffering, then we must be willing and ready to do the same. God never promised that we wouldn't face trouble, but He did say that we could take heart because He has already overcome the world.

"I have told you these things, so that in Me you may have [perfect] peace. In the world you have tribulation and distress and suffering, but be courageous [be confident, be undaunted, be filled with joy]; I have overcome the world." [My conquest is accomplished, My victory abiding.]."
John 16:33 AMP

Now, just to be clear, there is a difference between the suffering we face due to a trial and the suffering we face when the Lord is disciplining us due to our sin. When we go through a trial, it is not because of anything we did wrong. You might have lost your job, got into a car accident, or found out that you have cancer due to no fault of your own, and you shouldn't blame yourself for what happened.

An example of this would be Job's story in the Bible. He was a blameless man who walked with God and in an instant, lost everything, from his livestock to his ten children. Reading through the book of Job allows us to see that God allowed that trial to occur, but a plan had been in motion to bring good out of that situation from the beginning. We also see that the Enemy had to seek permission from God to even attack Job in that way. This reveals the sovereignty of God and His ability to use even the attacks of Satan to fulfill His ultimate purpose in our lives. Aren't you glad you serve a God that can turn your lowest and darkest moments in life around for your good? We don't have to look far in Scripture to see similar occurrences happening. Think about the lives of Joseph, Shadrach, Meshach, Abednego, and Daniel. All of these men faced great challenges and obstacles, but they also experienced great victories because of their trust in God. In fact, their faithfulness to Him, in the middle of their circumstances, caused kings and entire nations to acknowledge the greatness and power of the Lord. This is the type of God that we serve; He is consistent in showcasing His glory through even the worst situations. Only God could take a negative situation and bring about a positive outcome. If the Lord was capable of doing it before, for these men and other individuals in the Bible, then He is capable of doing it now for us.

Can I let you in on a little secret? Just because you pray about something doesn't mean that it will turn out the way you imagined. And just because it doesn't turn out the way you imagined doesn't mean that God isn't in control. Sometimes, even after praying, fasting, and worshipping our way through, we are left with an outcome that leaves us wondering if He even heard us.

Maybe you lost a loved one, didn't get that job, had a miscarriage, or found out that your spouse is going through with the divorce. You cried out to God and stood on His promises, yet you were still left with a broken heart. I want you to be assured that the Lord does hear the cry of His people, He is in control, and He has the ability to turn even the ugliest situation around for His glory and your good. If you need to cry, then cry. If you need to go to counseling, then go to counseling. If you need to take time off, then take time off. Be real, open, and honest with the Lord, and other trusted individuals in your life, about how you feel. Just make sure that you don't let your temporary setback keep you from worshipping your ETERNAL God!

I know it's hard. I know it doesn't make sense. I know it hurts. But God is there to comfort, strengthen, and guide you. If you continue to seek Him, He will make sure that you come out of this stronger in your faith with a testimony that will point to the sufficiency of the Cross and His ability to make all things new!

Our God is sovereign, even when we go through the toughest moments of our lives. When we face hardship, He doesn't dip out on us and leave us to ourselves. He steps in like the Good Father that He is and provides comfort and strength. He sustains us, redeems us, restores us, encourages us, and saves us. We may not always understand why He allows certain things to happen, but one thing is sure—we can rely on the fact that He is FAITHFUL. We can trust that He's not caught off guard by what we are facing, and His eternal purposes are being worked even in our devastation. I know this is true because I have been in the midst of some of the hardest moments of my life yet had complete peace despite what I was going through. When I felt like a failure, God lifted me up and showed me that no matter what my circumstances looked like, I was His child.

Many have bought into the lie that, when life is good, God loves them and that, when life is bad, He doesn't. It may not always be expressed vocally, but there is a tendency for that thought to pop up in our minds. Why? It's the same trick that the Enemy has been playing on humanity since He convinced Adam and Eve that God was withholding something good from them in the garden of Eden. He whispers lies to get us to doubt God's love and goodness because He knows that the real battle lies in our minds. That's why it is so important to renew our minds with the Word of God (Romans 12:2) and to take captive every thought and make it obedient to Christ (2 Corinthians 2:5).

God has already proven His love for us through the sacrifice of His only Son! Putting our faith in Jesus and being adopted into His family does not make us exempt from going through hard times, but we do have hope. As God's children, we are now heirs of God and joint heirs with Christ. This means that we can trust that the trials and tribulations we go through will result in us being glorified together with Christ in eternity (Romans 8:16-17). So, whether we are having a bad day or a good day, God still loves us the same, and there's nothing we could do to change His mind.

Time to Reflect

1. How have you seen the sovereignty of God in the midst of your suffering?
2. Reflect on a time when God took a terrible situation in your life and brought good out of it. Then write it down and share your story with someone else.
3. Spend time in prayer asking the Lord to strengthen your faith so that when the next trial comes in your life, you will remain faithful and not waver.

"Who shall separate us from the love of Christ? Shall tribulation, or distress, or persecution, or famine, or nakedness, or peril, or sword? Yet in all these things we are more than conquerors through Him who loved us. For I am persuaded that neither death nor life, nor angels nor principalities nor powers, nor things present nor things to come, nor height nor depth, nor any other created thing, shall be able to separate us from the love of God which is in Christ Jesus our Lord."
Romans 8:35, 37-39 NKJV

15

DO NOT GIVE UP

> *"I would have lost heart, unless I had believed That I would see the goodness of the Lord In the land of the living. Wait on the LORD; Be of good courage, And He shall strengthen your heart; Wait, I say, on the LORD!"*
> Psalm 27:13-14 NKJV

I was ready to give up. I was without stable employment, without a permanent home, and with no idea of what God wanted me to do next, except to wait. I went from working a job that I enjoyed, teaching dance to young girls, to being unemployed. I lost my sense of purpose and direction. All I could do was pray, spend time with the Lord, and wait. I wanted desperately to apply for jobs, but every time I tried, I couldn't shake this feeling that I was running ahead of God. As I sat with God for hours and talked to wise counsel, it was pressed on my heart that God was redirecting my path and that I needed to be patient. Meanwhile, I felt like a complete failure.

I was trying to wait patiently on the Lord, and I don't know about you, but waiting patiently does not come easily for me. I can be patient when it is convenient for me, but when I'm waiting on an answer from God, it's easy for me to become anxious and want to run ahead and do my own thing. But then I think about stories in the Bible of people like Abraham and Sarah who rushed ahead of God's timing and had Ishmael, and I'm like, "Nope, I'm good!" (you can read about their story in Genesis 16). So, to cure my anxieties, I memorized Scripture and kept praying, "Lord, send me out into Your harvest." It was a rough time. I had little to no money, bill collectors were calling my phone like crazy, and I had no idea how my basic needs were going to be met. I couldn't shake this notion that God wanted me to rest and prepare for where He was taking me next. I would say, "I need money, Lord!" And He would say, "You need to trust Me. I have a plan."

I had a choice to either be patient and trust God or delay His plan coming to fruition by rushing ahead and "fixing" this my way. As the days turned into weeks, I still hadn't gotten much direction from the Lord about where He wanted me to go next except that it would involve youth. So, of course, I started looking up and applying for jobs at churches and other after-school programs but didn't hear anything back. Zero. Nada. I don't think I have sought God that much in my entire life. As I sat with Him hour after hour, He really began to shower me with love and opened my eyes to the unlimited love that Romans 8:35-39 talks about.

About two and a half weeks after losing my apartment, I was taking a walk with my best friend and her kids. As we crossed the street, The Holy Spirit pressed upon my heart that, when I came across the job that God had for me, I would know. I wouldn't have to second guess it, and it would be apparent that it was the job for me.

And that's exactly what happened.

A couple of weeks later, I remember leaving a prayer meeting and going to walk around my favorite lake in Dallas to pour out my heart to the Lord. I had been praying and fasting the day before, and although it had been a month since I had worked anywhere and my unpaid bills were piling up, I had hope that God was at work. The Holy Spirit began to reassure me that God had not forgotten about me and that His plan for me was still very much in motion.

I left with such a surreal sense of peace as I headed to a local bookstore to sit and apply for jobs. While browsing, I came across a listing for a position with a Christian non-profit that immediately jumped off the screen at me. As I read the description, I felt this deep sense of joy that this was what God had in store for me. I immediately applied for the position and began to praise God for whatever the outcome would be. One of the directors contacted me the next day to set up an interview for the following week, which only fueled my faith. The interview went well, and I was invited to come by the community center to learn more about the work they did and to meet some of the kids I would potentially work with.

And then, two weeks later, I was hired for the job!

I was completely shocked that God had given me this opportunity. I don't know about you, but it still blows my mind when God does exactly what He said He would do. I have those,

"What is man that you are mindful of him, and the son of man that you care for him? (Psalm 8:4)" moments quite frequently.

A lot of what the Lord taught me through His Word in those two months has proven useful in this current season. I couldn't see how getting evicted could have been a part of God's plan, but now, I'm thankful that He allowed it to happen. I learned to endure, to be compassionate, to love, to practice patience, to have faith, and to pray without ceasing in a totally new and deeper way. Not to say that I have arrived, but I do have a deeper intimacy with God that I do not believe could have been birthed any other way.

Since the first day of being at my job, I felt completely at peace. I know I am living out God's Kingdom purpose doing what He has called me to do. Some days have been super challenging, but the support I have from my co-workers and supervisors is incredible. The Lord has used various co-workers to heal me from a lot of the emotional scars I had from my past. It's the healthiest work environment that I've ever been in. Not only that, but the Lord even answered my prayer for mature men and women of God to disciple and help me grow in Him through my position. I will never forget when my first official staff meeting ended up focusing on the topic of the gospel. That was literally enough to make me shout, but how many of you know that we serve a God who does exceedingly and abundantly more than we could ever ask or think (Ephesians 3:20)?

I was hired as a part-time employee, but after only being employed for about three weeks, I was asked by the Executive Director of the non-profit to go full-time. I was astonished because that very morning in my prayer time, I had asked the

Lord to give me wisdom and discernment about another part-time work opportunity that I was thinking about taking. I had also prayed the year before that the Lord would lead me to full-time work in which I could mentor young girls, incorporate dance, make a decent salary, and have some health benefits.

This seemed too good to be true.

I am delighted to say that the Lord answered that prayer exactly according to my desires. It's been one of the most challenging and busiest seasons of my life, but it's such a sweet season as well. God truly turned the ashes of one of the most embarrassing seasons of my life and brought forth beauty from it. I went from being unemployed to having a full-time job in just six short months, and the Lord provided for my daily needs along the way.

I didn't get where I am today because of luck or chance but through prayer, seeking the Lord, walking by faith, and being obedient to Him despite the way things looked. It was His mercy and grace that sustained me. Now, I have no choice but to trust that God will continue to make a way. He has brought me this far, and I have faith that He won't leave me now.

I am here to encourage anyone who may be going through a season of hardship and tribulation. You are not alone, and God hasn't given up on you. Do not listen to the lies of the Enemy. The Word says:

"Therefore, since we have been justified by faith, we have peace with God through our Lord Jesus Christ. Through Him, we have also obtained access by faith into this grace in which we stand, and we rejoice in hope of the glory of God. Not only that, but we rejoice in our sufferings, knowing that suffering produces endurance, and endurance produces character, and

character produces hope, and hope does not put us to shame, because God's love has been poured into our hearts through the Holy Spirit who has been given to us."

Romans 5:1-5 NKJV

If you are a born-again believer, then you have The Holy Spirit living inside of you, and God is for you, not against you. His plan for your life will prevail. It may not look like what you imagined, but there is hope. God loves us enough to take us through storms to prune us, and nothing could ever separate us from His love.

"What then shall we say to these things? If God is for us, who can be against us? He who did not spare His own Son, but delivered Him up for us all, how shall He not with Him also freely give us all things? Who shall bring a charge against God's elect? It is God who justifies. Who is he who condemns? It is Christ who died, and furthermore is also risen, who is even at the right hand of God, who also makes intercession for us. Who shall separate us from the love of Christ? Shall tribulation, or distress, or persecution, or famine, or nakedness, or peril, or sword?"

Romans 8:31-35 NKJV

Seasons of transition, change, and loss are hard and uncomfortable, but it's in those seasons that a deeper dependency on God is developed. It's in those seasons that we truly see if our faith is genuine. It's in those seasons that we find out if we were seeking God for Him or simply for His stuff. The Lord is sovereign, and even the pain has a purpose when you are in Christ. It's sometimes hard for our limited minds to grasp, but His ways are not our ways. They are so much better.

I mentioned this before, but struggles don't always mean that you have sinned. Look at the life of Paul, who was imprisoned, beaten, and even shipwrecked for the sake of the gospel. Look at Jesus, who lived a perfect life but died on the Cross so that you and I could be reconciled back to God and enjoy fellowship with our Heavenly Father. As believers, we are not exempt from hardships, but we have access to divine help to get through them.

How you handle the storms of life show those around you if the God that you say you believe in is really real. It's an opportunity for God to get so much glory! Your feelings are real, and it's okay to have moments, but it's not okay to continually live in despair when you are a daughter or son of the Most High God. Your Father is GOOD, and you have reason to hope. This world and its struggles are so temporary, but our hope in God is eternal.

"The Spirit himself bears witness with our spirit that we are children of God, and if children, then heirs—heirs of God and fellow heirs with Christ, provided we suffer with him in order that we may also be glorified with him. For I consider that the sufferings of this present time are not worth comparing with the glory that is to be revealed to us."
Romans 8:16-18 NKJV

God sees every tear, every battle, and every struggle. He cares deeply. Don't run *from* Abba Father in your hard place; run straight into His arms. He's waiting!

Time to Reflect:

1. Ask God to give you His strength in any area of your life where you feel tempted to give up or have stopped trusting Him to come through.
2. Thinking of your history with God, in what ways could you encourage someone in your sphere of influence to not give up?
3. In what ways may God want to use your story and testimonies to encourage someone else to trust God more with their situation?

Part 7

FAITHFUL IN EVERY MOMENT

16

PRAYER: THE ULTIMATE LOVE LANGUAGE

*"It shall come to pass
That before they call, I will answer;
And while they are still speaking, I will hear."
Isaiah 65:24 NKJV*

When I was a child, I demonstrated my love for others by making cards for people. It didn't matter what the occasion was. I would carefully pick out the right color of construction paper and spend hours using crayons, markers, and scissors to make the perfect card for my loved ones. From birthday cards to Christmas cards, my family knew that if it was a special occasion, they would be receiving a handmade card from me. Even though I spent a lot of time preparing, creating, and deciding what to write in the cards, none of that mattered once it was time to present them with their gift. I loved seeing the reactions on their faces when they received my cards. All the hours spent working seemed small and trivial.

I cannot help but think that must be how God looks at us. He prepares and plans things for us in anticipation of how we will receive them. The Lord does not do things haphazardly; He does things intentionally. Yes, He is a just and righteous Judge that will not tolerate sin, but He is also gracious, kind, and merciful. He's a Father who loves to hear from His children and answer when they call out to Him. I expressed my love as a child by making handmade cards on special occasions, but God expresses His love by showing up in the details of our lives every single day.

Have you ever thought about prayer being an act of love? One day, as I was writing in my journal, it hit me like a ton of bricks. What is the one thing that people who are in love do all the time? Talk! If we look at our relationship with God, we will see that, not only does He desire to spend time with us, but He also desires to communicate with us. Prayer is the channel through which a lot of this communication takes place. Every time we choose to go before His throne of grace, we are entering into the presence of the One who is love. Many of us tend to see prayer as a chore, an obligation, or a task to check off on our religious duty list. But what if we began to see prayer as an opportunity to express our love and thanksgiving to our Abba Father? What if we prayed His Word back to Him as if it were a love letter? The more we pray, the more we grow in our love for God. The more we seek Him, the more we find Him and begin to notice His sovereign hand at work.

PRAYER: THE ULTIMATE LOVE LANGUAGE

In my own journey of discovering the unfailing and unconditional love of God, it has often been through prayer that I have realized just how much He cares for me. It's the little things He does for me that might seem insignificant to everyone else that make my relationship with Him so rich. For example, in those moments when I cannot find keys, I stop to ask Him to show me where they are, and He provides when I find them five seconds later. Or I may be having a really hard day at work and ask Him for help, and then, my supervisor walks through the door to encourage and speak life into me. God also demonstrates His love through the way that He sends others to pray for us. Have you ever been frustrated or weary, and out of nowhere, God sent someone to encourage and pray for you? That was God's way of saying, "I see you; I love you; and I care about you." To think about how great God is and then to see Him answer prayer with such great detail has left me astounded multiples times. One of the things that I have learned throughout my journey with the Lord is that, not only does he love to provide for His children, but He also delights in surprising us.

If you know anything about my life, you need to know that God often calls me to take these big leaps of faith into the unknown. In my journey of walking by faith, God has really opened my eyes to see the importance of being specific in my prayers, to truly pray for things that seem impossible, and to pray more boldly—not just for myself—but for others as well. He has also been showing me just how much He is listening. I think sometimes it is easy to think that God isn't listening to us because we pray and nothing immediate seems to happen. Yet, when we pray, God does hear us and oftentimes has already begun to work things out in the spiritual realm. We must remember that it takes time for what has happened in the spiritual realm to occur in the natural realm. Sometimes, as we see in Daniel 10:12-14, there's a delay in our prayers due to the spiritual battle that is happening all around us. The angels are literally going to war against the Enemy on our behalf.

I don't know why sometimes, when we pray, the answers come immediately, and sometimes, when we pray, it takes hours, days, weeks, months, and even years for us to see a change. He's God, and He can do as He pleases when He pleases. The Lord doesn't operate on our timetable, yet His timing is ultimately perfect because everything that He does is good.

In her book *Set-Apart Femininity*, Leslie Ludy discussed the importance of persistent and specific prayer. She mentioned that a lot of times, we don't pray boldly or specifically for our needs because we don't truly understand the nature of our God. He is our Abba Father who delights in meeting the needs of His children and giving us good and perfect gifts. He loves showing up in the midnight hour and doing above and beyond all we could ask or think (Ephesians 3:20). On page 160 of *Set Apart-Femininity*[xviii], Ludy states, "God asks us to have the kind of faith that asks boldly for specific things. Instead of vague, general prayers that don't demand faith, we must begin 'putting it all on the line' and take the risk of laying our precise needs before our King."

I can recall a rough time in my life when I first moved to Texas that left me lonely and broken, but God showed up in a miraculous way. I didn't have a job, and it was weighing heavy on my heart. In my discouraged state, the Lord challenged me through a Bible study I attended one night to start praying more boldly and specifically. I imagined that, in order to help, God was sitting in heaven on His throne with His ear inclined to hear my requests. I was praying on a Saturday with my prayer partner, and I told her about the bill that had to be paid by the 17th of January in order for me not to get a late charge. Even though it was already the 16th, and I was a little over $120 short, she said she would stand in agreement with me that it would be paid. I figured that God could send whomever he wanted to provide me with the funds that I needed. I knew that the payment would not be taken out until at least Monday because it was the weekend. I logged onto the website after we prayed to pay the bill and was going to put the 18th as the payment date when the Holy Spirit prompted me to put the 16th instead. At the time, I didn't even realize the banks would be closed on Monday for the Martin Luther King, Jr. holiday, but clearly, God knew. A few moments later, I randomly checked my email, and someone had sent me $50 earlier in the afternoon! God was already starting to provide just like He said He would.

The next day, I went to visit a friend's church for Sunday service (which was good), but afterwards, I fell into a slightly depressed state. It was the first Sunday since I had moved, from Atlanta, that I did not have people to fellowship with after church. I suddenly missed everyone more than I had in over a week. I tried to cheer myself up by getting lunch and visiting a museum, but that didn't really help. For some reason, during the week, I was okay, but on Sundays, I missed my community back in Atlanta more than usual. Of course, as I called number after number, everyone I tried to reach out to didn't answer their phones. In my frustration, I went home and tried to take a nap.

    Later in the evening, I heard the Lord calling out to me, and honestly, I was so sad that I didn't even want to be bothered. I felt so alone and so lost. I had been crying out to God for community because I knew I needed accountability in this season, but it seemed like His ears were deaf to my cry. I sensed the Lord calling out to me again, inviting me to pour out my heart to Him. This time, I couldn't resist, and I immediately began to tell Him everything—how alone I felt and how I just needed some hope. I was trusting Him to come through in so many ways, and as each day went by, I felt my hope dying out and worry increasing in my heart. I was trying to pray, but it seemed useless, and I was just plain ole tired from fighting to believe that God was hearing my pleas. After I was completely finished voicing my deepest fears, worries, and concerns, the Lord responded by asking me what He could do to help me trust him more in this journey. I said, "If someone gave me $100-$200—" but cut myself off. I remembered what I had been studying about not only being specific but praying with bold faith. I had already seen God send people to give me $100, so that would take zero faith. It was time to take it up a level.

    I responded by saying, "If someone gave me $200, then I would feel as if you are hearing me." He said, "Okay," and I went about my evening. I couldn't believe what happened next. That same night someone reached out to me and sent $100! I was able to go get groceries and put the remaining money towards the bill. I still didn't have enough, but I knew at the very least I could go withdraw a cash advance from one of my credit cards if I needed to.

When I woke up the next morning, I was worried all over again because I never addressed the issue at-hand. Instead of sitting in the Lord's presence and studying His Word like I should have the night before, I watched a movie. One of the women from my dance ministry back in Atlanta had shared her testimony in our group chat about how God had come through for her, and it encouraged me to sit at the feet of Jesus. I started off by repenting for trying to run to everything and everyone else for comfort instead of seeking Him. I confessed my unbelief and cried out to Him about everything else that was on my heart. I just remember saying over and over, "I need you God; I need you God; I need you God. I need a community; I need a sense of purpose in this season, and I need provision. I want to trust You more."

There's something about being transparent with the Lord that is so freeing and brings so much joy and peace. It didn't even matter when or how God would do it; I had the reassurance I needed that God was for me and had a plan for my crisis. After my quiet time was over, I just happened to check my email again, and someone had sent me $300 (*cues organ and goes running around the room and jumping up and down*)! I didn't know the person, nor had I even solicited help from anyone else.

My God, My God, My God!!!!

Not only did He answer my specific request, He truly went above and beyond!!! I was so excited that I shared this testimony on my Facebook page:

I am a witness that God will do exceedingly above all we can ask or think!!!!! Because of that generous donation now all of my bills for the rest of the month will be covered, plus gas & groceries!!!! I cannot even comprehend God's faithfulness and have never experienced anything like this in my life before!!!! Nothing is impossible for Him!!!!! A big thank you to everyone who has obeyed the Lord and given to me. It truly has given me a reality of what the Bible describes in Acts when it says that the disciples gave so that everyone's need was met!!! Prayerfully, I'll be able to pay it forward one day!!!!

Later that day, someone else felt led to give me $30. Then, I went to a free Pure Barre fitness class, and they gave us $10 gift cards to Whole Foods Market. I was able to eat lunch for free as well. God is a provider! I had no idea when I was signing up for the class that I would get a free gift card, but God knew, which is why he placed it on my heart to go. And because of the holiday on Monday, the payment for the bill wasn't withdrawn until Tuesday, and by that time, all of the generous donations had successfully posted to my account.

He truly is an ON TIME God. To this day, this testimony brings a smile to my lips and joy to my heart as I think about God's faithfulness to answer prayer. When I'm tempted to think that God has forgotten about me, I recall this and other times when He showed up and showed out in my life to stir my faith to believe that He is bigger than anything I will ever face in this lifetime. And the same goes for you as well.

PRAYER: THE ULTIMATE LOVE LANGUAGE

Time to Reflect:

1. Have you been praying general or bold, specific prayers to God?
2. Ask God to reveal any areas of your life where you have placed limitations on Him in your prayer life.
3. Write down three things that you need God to do for you and over the next seven days; when you pray, be specific in your requests.

"And we are confident that he hears us whenever we ask for anything that pleases him. And since we know he hears us when we make our requests, we also know that he will give us what we ask for."
1 John 5:14-15 NLT

17

MOVING FORWARD

"All praise to God, the Father of our Lord Jesus Christ. God is our merciful Father and the source of all comfort. He comforts us in all our troubles so that we can comfort others. When they are troubled, we will be able to give them the same comfort God has given us. For the more we suffer for Christ, the more God will shower us with his comfort through Christ. Even when we are weighed down with troubles, it is for your comfort and salvation! For when we ourselves are comforted, we will certainly comfort you. Then you can patiently endure the same things we suffer. We are confident that as you share in our sufferings, you will also share in the comfort God gives us.
2 Corinthians 1:3-7 NLT

It's not about us.
    The hardships, suffering, and affliction that we face serve a greater purpose in God's plan. The Lord allows us to experience those obstacles so that we may be able to minister to someone else who is experiencing a similar event in their own lives. It is about Christ and His power being revealed through

us to someone we may or may not even know yet. As Christ comforts us in our place of hardship, we are able to comfort one another. We can testify to the person who was abused by their father that God is a healer, restorer, and redeemer. We can testify to the person who was abandoned by their mother at a young age that God still has a plan and purpose for their life. We can testify to someone who had an abortion that God is a God of second chances, a God who offers forgiveness, and a God who removes all guilt and condemnation. We can testify to someone who is struggling in their marriage that God is a reconciler.

We naturally tend to cry out, "Why me, Lord?" when faced with a hard situation, but I want to challenge you to change your perspective. What if we looked at suffering as an opportunity for us to show someone else that God is good and that His love is relentless, even in the midst of a storm? We go through what we go through to help someone else get through what we went through. The more intense the suffering, the greater the opportunity for God to be glorified.

Now, I'm not saying that we should go out and create our own opportunities to experience affliction. However, I am saying that we need to trust that God's love will sustain us, and we need to look for ways to give Him the glory and honor He deserves. Someone is always watching your life, even though you may never be aware of it. We serve a God who is very strategic and places us amongst certain groups of people in order to impact their lives. We are called to be His ambassadors (2 Corinthians 5:20), which means that we have a responsibility to represent Christ well amongst others—both non-believers and believers alike. The

Lord desires for everyone to be saved and come to the knowledge of truth (1 Timothy 2:4).

While it is the work of God to draw men to Himself, we still have a part to play in God's desire to reveal Himself to mankind. As I mentioned earlier, ministry is not just done in a pulpit on Sunday mornings or Wednesday evenings. There are opportunities to minister to others at your job, the park, the grocery store, bank, Target, the mall, the airport, and wherever else you may step foot throughout the week. It's why Paul tells us in 1 Peter 3:15 (NASB),

"…but sanctify Christ as Lord in your hearts, always being ready to make a defense to everyone who asks you to give an account for the hope that is in you, yet with gentleness and reverence."

In order to be able *"to give an account for the hope that is in you,"* you must first have that hope within and be ready to share why. Could you imagine how radically different our lives would look to unbelievers if we lived out that one verse?

I can't help but think of a scene from the movie *War Room* when I read that Scripture. In that scene, Elizabeth Jordan is in the bedroom with her husband when he tells her that he has just lost his job. He's expecting her to blow up, yell, and get upset, but instead, she stays calm and encourages him. Why? Because she trusts God and believes in the power of prayer. Her response actually causes her husband to take notice that something is different in her, and eventually, he ends up sharing her same faith.

When I went through my eviction in 2016, many people had no idea. From the outside, you would never have been able to tell that I was going through one of the roughest seasons of my life. It was not because I was trying to put on an act, but it was because I was spending hours in my prayer closet with God asking Him for strength, peace, hope, and faith to believe that my situation would not always look the way it did. People were shocked when I asked them to pray for my needs in that season because my demeanor did not match what I was going through. I was struggling to get by and many times, wanted to quit, but God sustained me.

Some days, I barely had enough gas in my car to get to the grocery store, and once I got there, I only had a few dollars to my name. But I had no choice other than to trust God to be *Jehovah Jireh* (My Provider). I saw the Lord come through for me in many amazing ways in that season, and it makes where I am today so much sweeter. I know what it's like to have nothing and to have debt collectors calling you every ten minutes, and I know what it's like to be able to put your bills on auto-pay with the confidence that you have exactly what you need to cover the payment.

I was able to minister to so many people who were facing similar trials and tribulations during that time in my life. Because I had been completely stripped of any self-sufficiency, the only person whom I could point them to was Jesus. The only hope and comfort that I could offer them was the same hope and comfort that Jesus was giving me daily. Though I felt unstable, insecure, and uncertain of what each day would hold, I do not think I have ever been as close to God as I was in that season. If God were to rewind my life and say that I had an option to rewrite that part of my life, I would do it all over again because I learned things about God and witnessed miracles that I never want to forget.

God has an eternal purpose for what He allows to happen. We may never get an explanation for the shootings, natural disasters, and social injustices that happen in this world, but God's love is unchanging. He may not always be the One directly causing the incident, but the Lord can surely use it to bring about good. We live in a world that is full of sin and because of it pain, injustice, darkness, and evil are the consequences of humanity's rebellion against God. However, I fully believe that there are some evils that the Lord wants to partner with us to override. God may allow these works of evil or disaster so that His Church may rise up and take action to be a light in the midst of darkness.

We know that evil is rampant in our society, but I want to remind you that this is not the end for God's children. We are awaiting the return of our Lord and Savior, Jesus Christ. Even on the hardest days, we can have hope that, because of God's love for us, He has made it possible for us to spend eternity with Him. In the meantime, let us devote our lives to bringing glory to Him and being intentional about making disciples whose faith is built on the truth of God's Word. He didn't have to choose us, but He did. And that alone deserves a hallelujah praise.

After reading the words written in these pages, my prayer is that you now have a better understanding of God's unfailing and unconditional love for you. I pray that many of the myths you have believed about God and His love have been dispelled through the chapters of this book. I pray that you have come to a better understanding of just how important it is to combat the lies of this world, our flesh, and the Enemy with the truth found in God's Word. I pray that you have been encouraged to go deeper in your walk with God and not to give up when things get hard. I pray that, through this small glimpse into my life and the work that God has done and is doing, you have been comforted to know that you are not the only one who has doubts at times. I pray that you will share the truth with someone else because the world needs to know and understand the true meaning of love. The world needs to know that our God is completely in control and can be trusted.

We truly do serve a good Father whose love is not based on what we deserve or anything we do, but it is based solely upon His grace. It's not about how you started, where you started, or even when you started. It's about responding to the truth, receiving His love, and walking in it. Remember, God is not looking for perfect people. He is looking for individuals who recognize that, apart from Him, they will never be righteous enough to save themselves, and they are willing to follow Him. Jesus is the only way to reconcile with the Lord and inherit eternal life. We can't do anything to earn His love because it is a free gift. I implore you to receive His grace and walk in the light of His love. Surrender what you think God is like and allow Him to show you what He is like through His Word and the Holy Spirit.

It's not enough for us to hear about His love; we must experience it. The best part about it is that He's waiting, willing, and desiring to reveal the depth of His love for you. I've shared a little piece of my journey with you, and now it's your turn. Share your story and how Christ has changed your life with someone else.

Scripture tells us that we overcome by the blood of the Lamb and the word of our testimony (Revelation 12:11). For many years, I was ashamed to tell my story because it didn't seem dramatic enough. I didn't have a story that seemed impressive like when people get up in front of a group and say stuff like, "I used to be a drug addict, alcoholic, and stripper, but Christ has set me free." In my eyes, those stories were way better than mine, which consisted of more internal battles that weren't very visible to the outside world. What the Lord has shown me is that every story is unique, and every story is needed. Whether your struggle is internal, external, or both doesn't matter. What matters is the fact that God changed you and is changing you into His likeness, which is something that you could never do on your own. There's a hurting and dying world that is searching for love in all of the wrong places, and you have the answer in Jesus.

Don't be timid.

Don't be afraid.

Be bold and courageous, knowing that God has already gone before you (Deuteronomy 31:8). You may be holding the key to someone's deliverance, salvation, breakthrough, or healing through the power of the Holy Spirit that is working in you.

I want to declare and pray this passage of Scripture over your life,

"I pray that from his glorious, unlimited resources he will empower you with inner strength through his Spirit. Then Christ will make his home in your hearts as you trust in him. Your roots will grow down into God's love and keep you strong. And may you have the power to understand, as all God's

people should, how wide, how long, how high, and how deep his love is. May you experience the love of Christ, though it is too great to understand fully. Then you will be made complete with all the fullness of life and power that comes from God."

Ephesians 3:16-19 NLT

Thank you for taking this journey with me. May God bless you richly.

And remember: God loves you unconditionally.

NOTES

[i] Evans, Tony. "*Understanding God's Love.*" August 7, 2019. Oak Cliff Bible Fellowship Church, Dallas, Texas. YouTube, 40:27. https://www.youtube.com/watch?v=qnUlz1zHM3s&t=1478s.

[ii] *The Merriam-Webster.com Dictionary*, s.v. "love (*n.*)," accessed November 15, 2018, https://www.merriam-webster.com/dictionary/love.

[iii] Wagner, Jerry. "*The Misunderstanding of Forgiveness.*" Speech, Disciple City Church, Dallas, TX, April 21, 2019.

[iv] Catron, Adrian. "What Is Love? A Philosophy of Life." *HuffPost*, The Huffington Post, 7 Dec. 2017, https://www.huffpost.com/entry/what-is-love-a-philosophy_b_5697322.

[v] Burton, Neel. "These Are the 7 Types of Love." *Psychology Today*, Sussex Publishers, 25 June 2016, https://www.psychologytoday.com/us/blog/hide-and-seek/201606/these-are-the-7-types-love.

[vi] *The Merriam-Webster.com Dictionary*, s.v. "identity crisis (*n.*)," accessed August 26, 2018, https://www.merriam-webster.com/dictionary/identity%20crisis.

[vii] Morrison, Toni. *The Bluest Eye*. New York: Vintage Books, 1970.

[viii] Desiring God. Accessed 5 February 2018. https://www.desiringgod.org/topics/identity-in-christ.

[ix] Hart, Joshua, et al. "Attachment Theory as a Framework for Explaining Engagement with Facebook." *Personality and Individual Differences* 77 (2015): 33–40. doi:10.1016/j.paid.2014.12.016.

[x] Gregoire, Carolyn. "It's True: We Use Facebook To Feel Better About Ourselves." *HuffPost*, The Huffington Post, 10 Feb. 2015, https://www.huffpost.com/entry/facebook-insecurity_n_6652128.

xi American Society of Plastic Surgeons. "More than $16 Billion Spent on Cosmetic Plastic Surgery." *American Society of Plastic Surgeons*, American Society of Plastic Surgeons, 12 Apr. 2017, https://www.plasticsurgery.org/news/press-releases/more-than-16-billion-spent-on-cosmetic-plastic-surgery.

xii *The Merriam-Webster.com Dictionary*, s.v. "bondage (*n.*)," accessed July 27, 2018, https://www.merriam-webster.com/dictionary/bondage.

xiii Mints, Paul. "*Evangelism.*" Speech, Initiative Network 72 Training Day, Dallas, TX, December 16, 2017.

xiv *New Oxford American Dictionary*, 3rd ed (2010), s.v. "Promise."

xv Smietana, Bob. "Americans Are Fond of the Bible, Don't Actually Read It." *LifeWay Research*, Lifeway Research, 23 Aug. 2017, https://lifewayresearch.com/2017/04/25/lifeway-research-americans-are-fond-of-the-bible-dont-actually-read-it/.

xvi "*New Oxford American Dictionary*, 3rd ed (2010), s.v. "Refuge."

xvii "*Come, Thou Fount of Every Blessing*," Public domain.

xviii Ludy, Leslie. *Set-Apart Femininity*. Oregon: Harvest House Publishers, 2008.

ABOUT THE AUTHOR

Cierra Rebekah Cotton, a native of Baltimore, MD, is an author, blogger, speaker, dancer, and mentor, who currently resides in Dallas, Texas. She graduated in 2007 from the prestigious, Baltimore School of the Arts with honors in dance. Cierra also trained at The Ailey School & graduated in 2011 with honors from Fordham University, in New York City, with a B.F.A. degree in dance. Since then, she has worked as a dance educator for over seventeen different schools & organizations across five different states.

Prior to moving to Dallas, she also spent time in Atlanta, GA, where she served in leadership as the director of a women's and dance ministry for a newly planted church. It was in Atlanta that Cierra's heart for ministry and people was ignited and she discovered her calling to teach, write, and speak. Her journey of faith, commitment to presenting God's Word in an accurate and relatable way, and refreshing transparency, has inspired many others to follow after God wholeheartedly. Cierra has a heart for serving youth and currently works with inner city students, through a non-profit organization called Behind Every Door Ministries. She desires for young people and women to know their value and identity in Christ, become who God has destined them to be, and rise up to be leaders in their community.

To read Cierra's blog, stay up to date with her, and learn more about the work that she is doing visit www.cierrarebekah.com or follow her on Instagram: @cierra_rebekah.